WHEN GOD SHOWS UP

by ROBERT NOLAND

40 DAY DEVOTIONAL

BroadStreet
PUBLISHING

Published by BroadStreet Publishing Group, LLC
Racine, Wisconsin, USA
www.broadstreetpublishing.com

WOODLAWN—WHEN GOD SHOWS UP

Written by Robert Noland and published in association with the literary agency, WTA Services LLC, Franklin, TN

ISBN: 978-1-4245-5088-3 (hardcover)
ISBN: 978-1-4245-5089-0 (e-book)

Cover design by Chris Garborg at www.garborgdesign.com
Interior typesetting by Katherine Lloyd at www.TheDESKonline.com

Stock or custom editions of BroadStreet Publishing titles may be purchased in bulk for educational, business, ministry, fundraising, or sales promotional use. For information, please e-mail info@broadstreetpublishing.com.

Printed in China.

15 16 17 18 19 20   5 4 3 2 1

CONTENTS

Introduction 5

Day 1   Cut to the Heart 7

Day 2   Only One Explanation 11

Day 3   End Zones & Comfort Zones 15

Day 4   Battling Boundaries. 19

Day 5   A House Divided 23

Day 6   Dialing Down Differences 27

Day 7   Enter—ruptions 31

Day 8   The Finer Points of Persistence 35

Day 9   But Everything to Gain 39

Day 10   The Bond of Belief 43

Day 11   From Bleachers to Battlefield 47

Day 12   God's Growth Gauges 51

Day 13   Spirit Speak. 55

Day 14   Discover Divine Destiny. 59

Day 15   The Faith Factor 63

Day 16   The Fire of Faith 67

Day 17   Confidence is a Contact Sport. 71

Day 18   The Reach of Speech 75

Day 19   Living on the Fault Line 79

Day 20   Rise Up & Run Strong 83

Day 21   Called & Courageous. 87

Day 22	On This Day!	91
Day 23	New Day, New Life	95
Day 24	Of Blood & Water	99
Day 25	The Father's Heart	103
Day 26	Message Manifesto	107
Day 27	If You Want God	111
Day 28	Faithful in a Fallen World	115
Day 29	Time to Call "Time Out"	119
Day 30	Risk, Reward & Reassurance	123
Day 31	Makin' Space for Grace	127
Day 32	Eternal Exchange	131
Day 33	Courage vs. Cowards	135
Day 34	Friday Night Lights	139
Day 35	When God Shows Up	143
Day 36	Father Favor	147
Day 37	Speaking Your Heart	151
Day 38	Goal–Line Glory	155
Day 39	Miracle Moments	159
Day 40	Leaving a Lasting Legacy	163
	When God Shows Up—In Your Life!	167
	About the Author	169

INTRODUCTION

Mark 1:35 tells us Jesus got up early in the morning and went away alone to pray. One of the most life changing spiritual disciplines in which you can invest is a daily and dedicated time alone with God. No distractions. No devices or noise and no one else around. Here are a few steps for success in utilizing this book:

1. Decide to commit. Purpose to use this book for the next forty days, one day at a time. Set aside the time to make a habit of engaging with the words contained here. If you miss a day, just pick back up. Don't quit. Commit.

2. Pick a time. While spending time with God first thing in the morning is best to set the pace for your day, choose a time that is optimum for your schedule. You may need to experiment a bit, but pick a time and stick with it.

3. Choose a place. You need a quiet and peaceful setting. Get away from distractions. Turn off the phone. The place is crucial for you to be focused and comfortable as you engage with God.

4. Read. Take in the content—every word. Carefully read the Bible verses. If you prefer to use your own version of Scripture each day, feel free to do so.

5. Journal. To answer the closing questions and open-ended statements at the end of each day, consider using a journal or notebook during these forty days. Write out anything you hear from God or feel you need to express from the challenge given. Journaling is a powerful tool God can use to help you process your spiritual walk.

6. Pray. Allow time to speak with God and tell him everything as you would a best friend. If you have never spent time in personal prayer, the next forty days could revolutionize your spiritual growth.

7. Listen and obey. Close your time with a quiet moment to hear God speak. Then obey what you hear and "walk out" what He tells you each day. The goal is to complete these forty days and allow Jesus to change your life!

> "Here's what I want you to do: Find a quiet, secluded place so you won't be tempted to role-play before God. Just be there as simply and honestly as you can manage. The focus will shift from you to God, and you will begin to sense his grace" (Matthew 6:6 MSG).

CUT TO THE HEART

The setting is the Cotton Bowl in Dallas, Texas. The iconic football arena is filled to capacity with an estimated 100,000 young people. An evangelist, standing on the platform, voice echoing through the sound system, calls out, "Let this moment be the spark of a spiritual fire that will sweep all over this land. This is a desperate generation, void of hope and meaning. A generation begging for something more than the life they are now living!" He pauses a moment, then boldly states to the crowd, yet as if he were face-to-face with each individual, "What are you gonna do about it? Change begins with you!"

The minister's message sounds so current, so relevant to this culture, so on target for today, but when this scene actually took place might surprise you.

The year was 1972—the peak of the "Jesus Revolution." The event was Explo '72, sponsored by Campus Crusade for Christ. The evangelist who spoke those words was Wales Goebel. Billy Graham also spoke. Johnny Cash sang. Revival had broken out in the land. Young people, proudly known as "Jesus Freaks," had converged en masse on the Texas landscape in the blistering summer heat.

Here's another scene, another crowd, another powerful moment led by an evangelist.

Jews from every nation were gathered in Jerusalem for Pentecost. Suddenly, a sound like a violent wind swept through one particular house. The Holy Spirit, the One Jesus had promised to His disciples, had come. The crowds nearby heard this strange noise so, bewildered and curious, they began to assemble nearby. Then a quite intriguing occurrence took place. They began to hear their native tongues being spoken—many languages, simultaneously, with a message of redemption and hope.

Scripture says that "Parthians, Medes, Elamites; residents of Mesopotamia, Judea and Cappadocia, Pontus and Asia, Phrygia and Pamphylia, Egypt and the parts of Libya near Cyrene; visitors from Rome (both Jews and converts to Judaism); Cretans and Arabs" all heard the wonders of God declared in their own tongues. Amazed by this miracle, they began to ask, "What does this mean?" (Acts 2:9–12 NIV).

Peter, the impulsive and impetuous disciple who had taken a sword to the guard's ear in the garden and denied Jesus in the courtyard, boldly stood to speak. He quoted from the prophet Joel and then explained in detail about Jesus' mission. Take a look at his conclusion and the culmination of his message in Acts 2:36–41:

> "Therefore let all Israel be assured of this: God has made this Jesus, whom you crucified, both Lord and Messiah." When the people heard this, they were cut to the heart and said to Peter and the other apostles, "Brothers, what shall we do?" Peter replied, "Repent and be baptized, every one of you, in the name of Jesus Christ for the forgiveness of your sins. And you will receive the gift of the Holy Spirit. The promise is for you and your children and for all who are far off—for all whom the Lord our

God will call." With many other words he warned them; and he pleaded with them, "Save yourselves from this corrupt generation." Those who accepted his message were baptized, and about three thousand were added to their number that day (NIV).

Three thousand believed with one message! This was the start of the original "Jesus Revolution."

If you are a Christ follower, the result of that first sermon is the reason you know the gospel today. Verse 37 says, "When the people heard this, they were cut to the heart." Herein lies the root catalyst for true revival—people "cut to the heart" by the truth of God.

Can we still be "cut to the heart" in our self-absorbed culture? How might revival—the next "Jesus Revolution" take place today? … Or can it? Are we too far gone?

The answer lies in the evangelist's question to the Cotton Bowl crowd: "What are you gonna do about it? Change begins with you!" True revival saturates the hearts of people—one at a time—just like the message of Jesus did in that first century. A new Jesus Revolution can indeed happen today—starting with you.

Complete these open-ended sentences on your journal page:

We need a revival today because …

I need a personal revival in my life because … i'm tired of

Jesus, please "cut me to the heart" today by … running away from God.

When God shows up ...
a city can be saved.

ONLY ONE EXPLANATION

The city of Birmingham, Alabama, became known as "Bomb-ingham," after suffering over fifty bombings since 1947, due to racial tension.

Martin Luther King called Birmingham "the most thoroughly segregated city in the United States."

On June 11, 1963, Governor George Wallace stood in the doorway of The University of Alabama, vowing that the school would never integrate.

Amid much controversy, Alabama football coach Paul "Bear" Bryant invited USC's fully integrated team to play in Birmingham on September 12, 1970.

Tandy Gerelds, the head coach at Woodlawn High School in Birmingham at the height of the segregation and bussing battle, reflects, "If you'd have asked me in 1973 if I believed in miracles, I'd a-said, 'Absolutely not.' I'd a-told you that it's a brutal world out there and my only comfort in it is that I am the master of my own fate. I'm the captain of my soul. Some people call what happened here in Birmingham a miracle. And there is only one explanation; only one way any of this could have happened."

We humans are contradictory creatures when you consider we want so desperately to believe in something or someone bigger than ourselves, yet are so doubting and distrusting all at the same time. Literally, walking contradictions.

The one thing no one can argue or debate is a life God has forever changed. Living proof is hard to explain away when, as Coach Gerelds declared, there is "only one explanation."

When anyone asked the apostle Paul to explain what happened in his life he might have also said, "There is only one way any of this could have happened." When Paul was still Saul, he was not only the master of his own fate, but had taken it upon himself to decide the fate of many others as well. Imagine Ananias' crisis of belief when God told him to go find Saul of Tarsus—the murderer of Christians—to pray for him and his healing.

> But the Lord said to Ananias, "Go! I have chosen Saul for an important work. He must tell about me to those who are not Jews, to kings, and to the people of Israel. I will show him how much he must suffer for my name. So Ananias went to the house of Judas. He laid his hands on Saul and said, "Brother Saul, the Lord Jesus sent me. He is the one you saw on the road on your way here. He sent me so that you can see again and be filled with the Holy Spirit." Immediately, something that looked like fish scales fell from Saul's eyes, and he was able to see again! Then Saul got up and was baptized (Acts 9:15–18 NCV).

It's funny how we don't believe in miracles, until we experience one; how we question if God is real, until we cannot possibly deny His presence; and how we believe we are the master of our own fate, until we are backed into a corner with no answers.

If today your soul feels there has to be a deeper purpose to life, here's the good news: You long for truth, you have a sense of something more—because there is! Reading these words is not just random chance. Consider it your miracle. Today, you can meet the Jesus of the Revolution, the real Captain of your soul.

Christ didn't wait for you to come to Him. He died for your sin—disobedience to God—so that you wouldn't have to. He offers a home in His heaven, so the relationship you start today can continue forever. He is your "only One Explanation."

Are you ready for a new beginning? Consider praying this prayer:

Lord Jesus, thank You for dying for my sin, rising again to defeat death and hell, and for entering into my life to live forever. I surrender to You now. I give my heart, mind, gifts, and talents for You to use as You see fit, from this day forward. Make my life all You want it to be—my "only one Way."

If you prayed that prayer, in your journal tell God your deepest thoughts in this important moment. Next, tell someone you know about your decision.

If you have prayed a prayer of salvation before, in your journal write down how you came to know Christ. Recalling your moment of salvation can be the fresh start of a new revival for you.

END ZONES
& COMFORT ZONES

In the heart of Birmingham, the last few fans are straggling out of the Crimson Tide's home stadium, after losing to USC 42 to 21. A lone figure in a checkered jacket and fedora hat leans against the south goal post, deep in thought. His players are slowly filing into the locker room. A reporter spots the opportunity to ask Coach Bear Bryant his take on the loss. He runs up to the sports legend and fires the first question: "What happened, Coach?" In classic Bryant fashion, he quips back, "We just got beat by USC. Weren't you payin' attention?" Undeterred, the reporter continues, "Why did you invite USC to Birmingham, Coach? You trying to make some sort of statement?" Bear is now done and just strolls away, straight into the *opposing* team's locker room.

As Bryant walks past USC's head coach, he yells to his team, "Gentlemen! Gentlemen! We have a visitor." The locker room gets eerily quiet, as everyone sees who has entered. Coach Bryant walks to the middle of the locker room and says, "If wanting to win is a fault, then I plead guilty. I like to win. I know no other way. It's in my blood. But when I get beat, I like it to be by an opponent worthy of my respect." He turns and walks over to Sam Cunningham, their star African American running back. Bryant puts out his hand and says, "Fine game, son. Brave of you to play it." Cunningham, as surprised as anyone, shakes his hand and responds, "Thank you, sir." The coach then says to the entire team, "Thank y'all for comin' down here."

As Bear comes out of the locker room, an assistant coach runs up to him. "Where you been, Coach?" "Talkin' to a real football player," Bryant answers. "Time and a place for everything. Ain't that what the Good Book says?"

The passage of Scripture to which Coach Bryant was referring is found in Ecclesiastes 3:1–8.

> Everything on earth has its own time and its own season. There is a time for birth and death, planting and reaping, for killing and healing, destroying and building, for crying and laughing, weeping and dancing, for throwing stones and gathering stones, embracing and parting. There is a time for finding and losing, keeping and giving, for tearing and sewing, listening and speaking. There is also a time for love and hate, for war and peace (CEV).

By Coach Bryant's walking in to meet Sam Cunningham in the opposing team's locker room, he could sense change in the air—for football, for Alabama, and for America. It was time to stop killing, destroying, weeping, and throwing stones. It was time to start planting, healing, building, gathering, and embracing a new paradigm. The winds of change were blowing and a new type of peace was approaching.

Change is a difficult proposition for the majority of people. We like our comfort zones. We like knowing exactly what is going to happen next. As a result, we get stuck in life. Some people get stuck for months, others for years, and some, unfortunately, for a lifetime.

So, how do you decide to venture out into new territory and declare it's time for change, like Bear Bryant? Here are a few practical helps:

1. **Don't mistake activity for productivity.**

2. **Don't ever lose your hunger for growth and change.**

3. **Wisdom from God is the only true catalyst toward constant change.**

4. **The only way to get unstuck is to move in a new direction.**

Isn't it interesting that the human condition will cause us to sit in one spot being miserable, because the risk to move creates a more overwhelming emotion—fear? Feeling a growing level of misery seems to numb the courage to risk. Often, until it's too late.

If you are moving forward, walking with God, and working alongside Him in the kingdom, stop and express gratitude today that you are living the abundant life. If you feel quite comfortable with where life is, watch out and ask for wisdom. If you know you are stuck, maybe it's time to ask God to help you escape the comfort zone.

Complete these sentences in your journal:

One place I feel I am growing and changing is …

One area I feel I am stuck is …

A place where I sense God calling me to change is …

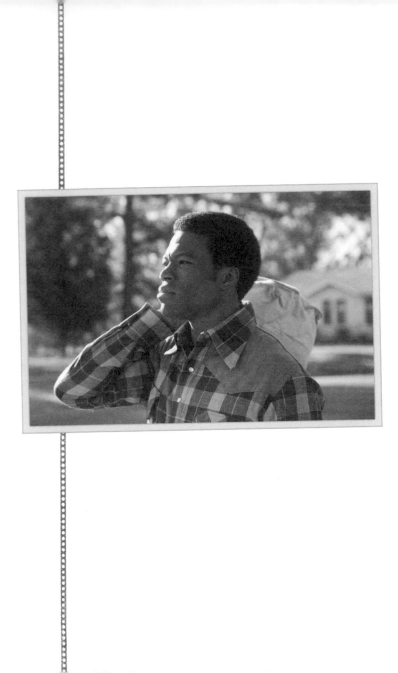

BATTLING BOUNDARIES

In 1973 at seventeen years old, Tony Nathan's six-foot-one, 190-pound frame is that of an obvious athlete. Cedric, his younger brother, protests, "I don't wanna go," talking about school. Tony empathizes with him, but reassures, "It's okay. Your school's not like my school." Cedric looks up and asks, "Will it ever be?" Tony stays silent, hoping Cedric never has to experience what he does on a daily basis at a school violently divided by forced segregation.

Just then Junior, Tony and Cedric's dad, enters, asking Tony, "Ready?" "Yes, sir," the young athlete answers. Tony gets in a morning run to school, while dad drives behind in the pre-dawn hour for security.

Tony takes off, followed by the car headlights of Junior, his son's constant support. He runs through his neighborhood, passing houses stacked within feet of each other in a poor but tight-knit African American community.

Tony runs across a bridge, representing far more of a divide than just geography. On the other side, he is in an all-white world. The houses are twice as large on this side. Everything about these streets feels competitive. Not as much "we're all in this together," but more "every man for himself." Finally, Tony runs through an industrial area and eventually into the parking lot of the school—Woodlawn High.

Junior pulls up to the school, tosses Tony his duffel bag, and then asks his son a very familiar question, "Tony, where you live from?" The young athlete smiles and holds his fist to his heart. "I love you, boy," his dad calls out.

This world has always had dividing lines. Some are created by geography and natural means, while others are invisible and unwritten. But everyone learns them by heart. We separate from each other by economics, race, politics, religion, education, and language—just to name a few. We are taught at an early age how to disconnect from one another into neat and tidy categories.

There was One Who walked the earth that paid no attention to the boundaries and borders humans draw. In fact, He constantly challenged and battled the limitations man created and enforced.

> Later, Matthew invited Jesus and his disciples to his home as dinner guests, along with many tax collectors and other disreputable sinners. But when the Pharisees saw this, they asked his disciples, "Why does your teacher eat with such scum?" When Jesus heard this, he said, "Healthy people don't need a doctor—sick people do." Then he added, "Now go and learn the meaning of this Scripture: 'I want you to show mercy, not offer sacrifices.' For I have come to call not those who think they are righteous, but those who know they are sinners" (Matthew 9:10–13 NLT).

The Pharisees and teachers of the Law had an issue with Jesus from the moment he stepped foot in their territory. Why? He crossed their boundaries. He blew past their borders. He would interact with anyone—good or bad, male or female, rich or poor, religious or irreligious.

When we follow Jesus, we commit to walk where He leads, not tiptoe the tightrope lines drawn by the culture. Like Tony's run through the segregated streets of 1970s Birmingham, our world is still just as divided today. But also like Tony's early morning run, crossing line after line, being followed lovingly by the watch care and light of his father, so are our lives in God's care when we only concern ourselves with His direction and path.

Representing Christ today, we work to add, not subtract—multiply, not divide—walking across the lines drawn by the world, so we can bring His message of hope and grace to everyone, anyone, who is ready to hear.

Junior's question and constant reminder to Tony is valuable to each of us to answer today: "Where do you live from?"

Complete these thoughts in your journal:

Heavenly Father,

I confess I have dividing lines in these places …

I feel as though people misjudge and treat me unfairly by putting me into this category …

My honest answer to the question "Where do I live from?" is …

Help me today to live from …

A HOUSE DIVIDED

As the Woodlawn football team fills the bleachers, the African American athletes are once again forced into the back corner of the stands. Their number has dwindled down to only a handful of players. Tony sits down beside his friend, Reginald Green, and scans the group.

The late-summer Alabama heat and humidity has everyone covered in sweat. Coach Tandy Gerelds, a stout man of five feet, ten inches with perfectly parted brown hair and a coach's uniform that reflects his focus and intentionality, steps into the gym with an air of dramatic flair. He stands stoically silent for what seems like an eternity, staring at the players, then he barks out, "Anger. ... I see it in your faces. You're angry because of what's happened to this school. ... Well, so am I. You feel hate, legitimate or not. ... So have I. You've been berated or beaten or shot at. ... Well, so have I. None of us chose this. It was forced on us. But we can choose together what we will do with it. So if it is anger that unites us, then let's use that anger to win, boys! 'Cause winning, ... well, it fixes just about everything, doesn't it?... Now, are there any questions? ... I didn't think so. Let's go do it."

There have always been two primary ways that kingdoms fall—explosion and implosion. External forces can threaten and attack, but many factors can cause inward erosion and ultimate failure. When the internal environment becomes hostile, one way to turn the tide is for that same energy to be focused together on an outside force, which is always where the real enemy awaits.

Once, when Jesus' miracles were being called into question, in particular the source of His power, He taught a very important principle, used and quoted often in religious, as well as secular settings. The verse found in Luke 11:17 states that a kingdom divided against itself will fall.

The New Living Translation expresses the verse this way:

"Any kingdom divided by civil war is doomed. A family splintered by feuding will fall apart."

Coach Gerelds was being bluntly honest about the team's circumstances with no other options than to face the stark reality head-on. The bigger picture had nothing to do with football. He realized the proper focus could change everything inside the team, so he confronted his players with the very difficult challenge of altering their perception and perspective.

Consider these three points of application, gleaned from Jesus' principle and Coach Gerald's speech:

1. In volatile circumstances, controlling the emotions of individuals may not be possible, but redirecting the corporate energy as fuel for change has great promise. Leaders for both good and evil have proven this concept repeatedly over the history of mankind by funneling anger and frustration into a movement. At Woodlawn, the players' obedience, coupled with God's Spirit, could make history for real change.

2. There is never a question of whether adversity will come, but only how one responds when it does. Existing in a broken and fallen world breeds problems and all manner of conflict. Living in the power of Christ allows us access to answers we otherwise would not have, as well as the supernatural boldness and strength to press onward in times of trouble.

3. Division leads to loss, while unity paves the path to victory. The Christian lifestyle will certainly bring some division as people reject Jesus in us, but as His people, we can be focused on unity as an ever-present opportunity.

Do you want to see the hand of God at work in your life in a powerful, unexplainable way? Confess anywhere your own house is divided. Be honest about the "civil war" that may be taking place in your own heart through anger, bitterness, shame, and the like. God already knows what you're going through, so just be honest with Him. His Spirit can bring unity to your soul, peace to adversity, and change to a divided life.

Complete these sentences in your journal:

Heavenly Father,

I confess my house is divided in these areas of my life ...

Please bring peace to my heart in these places ...

Where I need Your help the most to change is ...

When God shows up ...
battle lines will be broken.

DIALING DOWN DIFFERENCES

Mike Morton is the starting running back for Woodlawn. While he is a team leader, unfortunately, he rarely points the other players in the right direction. Running receiver drills, Tony lines up to cover him. Even in the shadows of the faceguards, the animosity in their eyes is obvious.

After looking like he has been beaten on the route, Tony catches up and leaps to intercept the pass. Reggie Green, Tony's buddy, calls out to Morton, "It's okay, Cupcake. That was just Superman flying over your head. It's not your fault." Mike responds by rushing Reggie to fight. In a flash, half the team joins in. Coach Stearns dives into the middle to break them up, yelling out, "Suicides! Sprints! Now! And you can thank these two for it!"

As the sun begins to set and the players are dragging, Coach Gerelds grabs Morton by the facemask. "This is your fault! Your fault, boy!" As he pulls him closer still, he keeps on, "Look at me! Where does your anger belong?! Who deserves it?!"

Morton knows full well what the coach means, so he grunts out, "Banks! Banks deserves it." Gerelds fires back, "That's right, our rivals across town, not your own teammate!" Then Coach calls out to the entire team: "This is what happens when you fight each other instead of fight to be a team!"

For quite a long time, the church in America has split

itself up into categories and subcategories, separating along deep dividing lines. Issues such as polity, worship elements and styles, missions, teaching approaches, baptism, and even splinter groups regarding the language used for the prayer of salvation, keep us separated. We have placed detailed focus on our differences.

Meanwhile, the Enemy of God has slowly eroded the culture—one issue at a time, one soul at a time, ever widening the path of destruction. While no one has been watching at the walls, the Enemy has been storming the gates, breaking through, and, too often, winning. To repeat the words of Coach Gerelds, "This is what happens when you fight each other instead of fight to be a team."

Consider Jesus' prayer to the Father regarding His heart for all those who would follow Him.

> "I am not praying for these alone but also for the future believers who will come to me because of the testimony of these. My prayer for all of them is that they will be of one heart and mind, just as you and I are, Father—that just as you are in me and I am in you, so they will be in us, and the world will believe you sent me.
>
> "I have given them the glory you gave me—the glorious unity of being one, as we are—I in them and you in me, all being perfected into one—so that the world will know you sent me and will understand that you love them as much as you love me" (John 17:20–23 TLB).

For revival to come, for the world to truly change, to turn the tsunami of evil that is engulfing our world, we must take our attention off the negotiable issues that divide us and look solely and only to the nonnegotiable One Who prayed this prayer for unity. If our eyes are affixed to Jesus, at least we are all focused in the same place, as well as the right place!

Of course, there are standards that Scripture makes clear we must adhere to as believers, but here we are talking about the petty differences of church membership, not the passionate doctrine of the church itself. As our beliefs and standards are attacked, our only correct response is to be a team once again—just as Jesus asked for us to become in His prayer. We must agree we can indeed line up together, fight toward the same goal, and hit the defense hard for the glory of God.

The great news is at the end of the Book, we win, so recruiting as many teammates as possible is our only goal. We can put aside our differences and fight as a team! God most certainly wants you to be a starter on His side so that "the world will believe."

Complete these sentences in your journal:

Lord, I confess I have gotten hung up on some petty differences in the body of Christ such as …

Father, help me to put aside my own differences by …

Dear Jesus, help me to keep my eyes on You today and influence my world by …

ENTER—RUPTIONS

Coach Gerelds is in his office, drawing out a "Power I" formation on paper. There's a knock at the door. Hank Erwin walks in, an energetic and optimistic ex-baseball player who also just happens to be a dreamer—the total opposite of Gerelds. The moment creates an immediate and awkward tension. "Hey, Coach. I'm Hank. I know you're a busy man, so I'll get right to the point. I'd like to have a meeting with your football team." The coach strikes a skeptical look and asks, "About what?" Hank matter-of-factly states, "Jesus Christ." Gerelds looks at him and laughs, "Oh. Wow. You some sort of preacher or something?" Hank answers, "No, I'm not a preacher. I'm a sports chaplain. I work with local teams in the area. Just moved here. I just wanna talk to your kids." Gerelds stares at him for a moment, then says, "Sorry, Hank, but you can't."

Hank pauses to try another approach. Gerelds, obviously now frustrated, asks, "You know this is a public school?" "Yeah, I know," he answers, well aware of where he is standing, then continues, "Look, I have seen things that are happening all over the country. Amazing things." "Well, you're not going to see them here," the coach states. Hank just keeps going, "I think your players could use it…. I think you could too." "Listen, Hank"—Gerelds sternly attempts to end the conversation—"if my team needs somethin', I'll tell you …" The coach grabs his cap, puts it on, and gives a final "we're done here" glance at Hank as he walks out the door.

> "So I tell you, ask, and God will give to you. Search, and you will find. Knock, and the door will open for you" (Luke 11:9 NCV).

While in the context of this verse, Jesus was teaching about persistence in prayer, inviting believers to engage in honest and constant conversation with the heavenly Father, there is also a principle here for the follow-up action of those prayers. Asking, searching, and knocking are proactive words. We should surely pray, but also then act on what God speaks to us from those prayers.

Hank Erwin had prayed diligently, just as this passage commands, regarding the Woodlawn football team, and God had told him in no uncertain terms to take Him to this team. How easy would it have been for Hank to inform God of how impossible the Woodlawn situation was and say no? Quite easy. How tempting do you think it was for Hank to tell God to get someone else to tackle this job? Very.

There are so many miraculous events in this world every day that take two catalysts to occur:

1. **A God Who is capable of producing miracles at will.**

2. **An obedient servant willing to carry out God's work on earth.**

Here's the very good news about these two points: Number one is covered! God is capable of producing miracles at His will. This is not a guarantee, of course, but assures us He in the business of bringing heaven to earth. The only question is now number two. Where will He find obedient servants?

If God were to speak to you today, would you have the capacity, the "bandwidth" available, to hear Him? The intention of this question is not to produce guilt, but an understanding that God wants to involve you—yes, you—in His work on earth. What an amazing opportunity!

Hank Erwin had to be willing to have an awkward moment, to be told no, to have a door slammed in his face, but he could endure this treatment because it wasn't about him—it was about God and his neighbors, the Woodlawn team.

We close today with Jesus' words from our passage: "So I tell you, ask, and God will give to you. Search, and you will find. Knock, and the door will open for you."

Complete these action points in your journal:

The main thing that tends to stand in the way of me hearing from God is ...

One area where I know I hear God clearly is ...

What is one thing you believe God has spoken to you to do where you can be involved with Him in His work?

When God shows up ...
        the faithful find favor.

THE FINER POINTS
OF PERSISTENCE

After another act of violence at the school and another meeting with the superintendant threatening his job and even closing the school, Coach Gerelds walks out of the principal's office to call his wife. As he is explaining he will, once again, be late coming home, he looks over and sees Hank Erwin with the principal and three African American students. The coach is immediately distracted and curious by the chaplain's presence.

As Gerelds gets off the phone, Hank approaches. "Hey Coach. Can I talk to the team now?" The principal begins to call for Gerelds to talk to the police. The coach impatiently tells Hank, "Look, I don't have time to deal with this now." As the principal calls louder for Gerelds, Erwin speaks up. "Coach! This is what I do. I help people." As the coach begins to walk away, he relents, "You know what—you have five minutes after training in the gym. You talk to Coach Stearns. You better be good."

Hank knew God had a plan and he clearly saw Coach Gerelds desperately needed one. Those factors drove him to connect the two.

In today's politically correct and I-don't-want-to-get-involved culture, this kind of persistence has become a dying art. Fear, apathy, laziness, and selfishness are the poor motivators of so many decisions today.

Because you know that the testing of your faith produces perseverance. Let perseverance finish its work so that you may be mature and complete, not lacking anything. If any of you lacks wisdom, you should ask God, who gives generously to all without finding fault, and it will be given to you (James 1:3–5 NIV).

Persistence and perseverance are closely related, but we often associate being persistent as focused on a task or goal, while perseverance as being more of a character quality in seeing things through in the long haul. Persistence in the short term often brings about perseverance for the long run.

To better understand God's brand of persistence, let's look at five R's.

1. Respectful. Persistence is often equated with being annoying, like the salesman who keeps following you through the store when you just want to look. His perseverance makes you want to do one thing—leave!

Hank didn't confront Coach Gerelds in front of the team; he spoke to him privately and personally. Persistence led by God will show respect to the other person or party.

2. Resourceful. Hank got to know first-hand the situation at the school and gathered information about his assignment.

Being resourceful is enacting and engaging wisdom into a situation to bring about the best scenario. God is the Creator and Ruler of all resources and can show you exactly what—and not—to use in any situation requiring persistence.

3. Realistic. Expressing faith doesn't mean we abandon logic and realism. Hank didn't just walk in and start preaching to the players. Could he have? Sure. Might it have worked? Maybe on a few guys. He mapped out the most realistic approach to be as efficient as possible.

4. Reciprocating. Many might say that persistence is just trying to get what you want. Too often today, people and relationships arc cither viewed as expendable or simply a means to an end.

God's way is always about the other person—"love your neighbor as yourself." Love constantly makes sure the road is clear for the other side as well.

5. Redeeming. God has an end goal in mind for His plans, to redeem people and situations, so the best may come about for everyone. In Hank's case, he knew God's end goal wasn't simply racial unity, ending violence, or even winning a game. Rather it was the redemption of souls with all these being the by-products. With God, it doesn't have to be either-or, but can often be both-and.

God's plans are well worth any effort we can faithfully give, because the end result is often amazing, even if we go through difficulties and trials to get there—through persistence *and* perseverance.

In your journal:

- Rate your everyday persistence level for all areas of life on a scale of one (lowest) to ten (highest).

- Rate your perseverance level for the kingdom of God on a scale of one (lowest) to ten (highest).

- Based on this honest evaluation, write down one thing you can do to improve your focus on the things of God.

BUT EVERYTHING TO GAIN

After finally finishing up all the meetings with the police and the principal regarding the day's violence at the school, Coach Gerelds locks up his office, and hears a voice coming from the gym. He walks in, surprised to find the meeting with the players is still going on.

A strange and reverent quiet has fallen over the players, as Gerelds hears Hank state, "I care about each and every one of you. I care about what you've seen. I care about what you've been through. I care about your pain. And so does God."

Gerelds walks over to Coach Stearns and says, "Jerry, what's going on? I said five minutes. It's been over an hour. We need to wrap this up." Stearns responds, "Tandy, hold on a minute. I know this sounds crazy, but let's give the guy a chance. We've got nothing to lose."

Erwin presses on, "I'm asking you to stand up right now, right here, and make a decision, to change, to forgive. To be forgiven. Because you are worth being forgiven. No matter what you've done. That's how much God loves you. I'm asking you to choose Jesus. Can you do that? Will you do that? With me? Right now."

Just as Coach Gerelds takes a step forward to stop Hank, Mike Allyson is the first player to stand up and walk forward. Then another player. And another. And another. Within a few minutes, most of the players are at the front—including Tony Nathan. Only Mike Morton and his buddies are still seated on the bleachers.

As Hank begins to pray, Gerelds, looking on in shock, asks, "What just happened?"

> Then Paul left the synagogue and went next door to the house of Titius Justus, a worshiper of God. Crispus, the synagogue leader, and his entire household believed in the Lord; and many of the Corinthians who heard Paul believed and were baptized (Acts 18:7–8 NIV).

When we read that almost every young man on the Woodlawn football team came to Christ, it is safe to say Coach Gerelds' "entire household believed in the Lord." God was most definitely up to something big at Woodlawn, just as he was in Corinth where Paul was speaking. The gospel was clear, hearts were ready, and people responded to the Truth.

Let's tie two important points together from both these accounts of God moving.

1. Hank didn't demand the team be taken to a church so he could preach to them. No. He came to them in the school gym. "Paul left the synagogue and went next door." Both men took the message to the people. Every day you encounter those that need to hear about Jesus, yet will never come to your church. For revival to come, we must take the message to the people, not wait on them to come to the messenger.

2. Hank Erwin could have been intimidated by the coaches and players—the entire volatile situation at Woodlawn—but he wasn't. Like Paul, he kept on speaking and was not silent.

For God to move in your circles of influence, you will have to take on the same response—have courage and speak.

Here is a very simple way to talk about your faith—your own story of what the Lord has done for you. In three to four sentences for each point, share:

… what your life was like before Christ.

… the circumstances of how you came to know Jesus.

… how a relationship with Jesus changed your life.

… something God is currently doing in your life today.

In your journal, write out your testimony using these four points as a guide. Recording it in a simple, concise form and rehearsing it a few times will help get you ready to answer the question, "What happened?" in your own life. Sharing your faith with people who feel they have nothing to lose can show them they have everything to gain.

When God shows up ...
     obedience builds bridges.

THE BOND OF BELIEF

Friday night just before game time—Woodlawn is playing Ensley. The players are in the locker room. Coach Gerelds, holding a newspaper, says, "*The Birmingham Post Herald* believes something about this team. They believe we're only going to win two games this year. They believe that this season is the death rattle of a school barely able to stay alive. You see, I don't believe this for a minute. I believe that we are the masters of our own fate. I believe that we can prove these people wrong. I believe that we can win. Why don't you go out there and show me what you all believe! Let's go and do it!"

Hank is standing next to Coach Stearns, looking downward, knowing Gerelds' speech about belief is good, but from the wrong motivation, as the team charges out to take the field.

The word "belief" is attached to so many connotations today. It can be a momentary emotion or a lifetime commitment—and all in between. Once when Jesus was teaching, he told a parable about a farmer who sowed seed on his land. Some fell on the road; other fell into gravel; some in the weeds; and some into the fertile earth. He then went on to explain the different places the seed fell represents people's hearts.

> "The seed is the Word of God. The seeds on the road are those who hear the Word, but no sooner do they hear it than the Devil snatches it from them so they won't believe and be saved.

"The seeds in the gravel are those who hear with enthusiasm, but the enthusiasm doesn't go very deep. It's only another fad, and the moment there's trouble it's gone.

"And the seed that fell in the weeds—well, these are the ones who hear, but then the seed is crowded out and nothing comes of it as they go about their lives worrying about tomorrow, making money, and having fun.

"But the seed in the good earth—these are the good-hearts who seize the Word and hold on no matter what, sticking with it until there's a harvest" (Luke 8:11–15 MSG).

We've all seen people believe, get really excited in the moment, and then, later, act like nothing ever happened. We've seen others, however, who capture a moment of faith that changes the course of their life forever.

God will provide the fertile ground we need to stay secured in our faith. The key is for us to "seize the Word and hold on no matter what, sticking with it until there's a harvest."

The Woodlawn players had all placed their faith and belief in Christ together. In his locker room speech, Coach Gerelds was challenging them to believe in themselves to prove others wrong. Hank was quietly challenging the team to a deeper level, to deeper soil—rooted, not in themselves, but in Christ. The only questions still remaining: Will it take hold? Will it last? Where will the "seed" fall for each young man on the team?

How does your life story track with Jesus' parable? Let today's truth—the good seed—fall on a fertile heart and bring renewal to your weary soul.

Complete the following in your journal:

- On a scale of one (lowest) to ten (highest), rate your spiritual walk in the season following your salvation.

- Using the same scale, rate your walk today.

- If you see you need to get back to a more committed place with the Lord, write down what you know you must do to get your life on the right path—where the good seed is found.

- *Heavenly Father, I want to "seize the Word and hold on no matter what, sticking with it until there's a harvest."* Please help me today to …

FROM BLEACHERS TO BATTLEFIELD

Woodlawn is playing Ensley. Tony, along with the other African American players, is on the bench. Tony's mom, known as Momma Nathan, yells out, "Play our boys! C'mon Tandy!" Soon the white parents are firing back in defense. The tension is escalating quickly.

Principal Owen Davis walks onto the sideline towards Gerelds and commands, "Tandy, I don't expect you to win, but I expect you to keep things quiet. ... Do something about this." Gerelds, visibly angry, fires back, "It's not my fault, Owen. I'm trying to coach football." "The principal leans closer and says, "Well, this is bigger than football, Tandy." He looks up to the divided and angry crowd as fathers from both the black side and the white side begin to get up and head toward each other. A fight is brewing.

Gerelds tells Coach Stearns, "Get Nathan." Stearns calls for Tony. Surprised, he jumps off the bench and runs to Gerelds, who says, "Safety. Go!" The parents, also shocked by the move, sit back down to watch. Crisis averted—for now.

Nervous, Tony glances at the stands, then back to the field, as Coach Stearns yells, "The slot, Nathan! Cover the slot!" The receiver takes off in front of him, going long, as Tony hears, "Pass! Pass!" He looks back over his shoulder to see the ball streaking through the air. He times his jump and, just like in practice, intercepts the ball!

Ensley players are barreling toward Tony as he begins to cut, running more side-to-side than down the field. As an opposing player hems him in, he goes out of bounds after thirty yards, but a lineman blindsides him with a late hit. Mike Allyson reaches to help Tony up and says, "Welcome to the game."

Coach Gerelds is in complete shock, but pleased the move worked. The parents all stay put. This moment would prove to be a huge turning point for Woodlawn.

Sometimes the game changers aren't in the starting lineup, but must be called up from the bench to the front to fight.

The Israelites were faced off against the Philistines. But there was a crisis in the ranks of the nation. Goliath, a nine-foot-tall giant, was standing every day and calling out, not only Israel, but also their God. King Saul and the military leaders didn't know what to do. Who could defeat this unstoppable enemy?

David is a shepherd boy who hears about the giant and the standoff. He tells Saul to put him in the game, because he can defeat him; he can intercept this bully. He runs out on the battlefield and lines up against Goliath. Let's take up there as David says:

> "Everyone assembled here will know that the Lord rescues his people, but not with sword and spear. This is the Lord's battle, and he will give you to us!" As Goliath moved closer to attack, David quickly ran out to meet him. Reaching into his shepherd's bag and taking out a stone, he hurled it with his sling and hit the Philistine in the forehead. The stone sank in, and Goliath stumbled and fell face down on the ground (1 Samuel 17:47–49 NLT).

Crisis averted. But a most unlikely hero is introduced into history. David, like Tony, is a game changer. Even though Saul and Coach Gerelds weren't at all confident of the possible outcome, the risk of an unknown player paid off.

There will be times in our lives when we will look back and see those game-changer moments. At the time, they were surprising, often terrifying, but they alter the course of life from that moment on.

Is there a Goliath in your life right now?

Is there a "giant" problem attacking you?

Are you sitting on the sidelines, but ready to take the field?

Are you sitting on the bench, afraid of the game where the giants are playing?

Regardless of your situation, repeat David's words to encourage yourself today: "This is the Lord's battle and He will give it to me."

Complete these sentences in your journal:

The situation where I am facing the most controversy or opposition right now is …

The place where I feel the most pressure to perform or save a situation is …

God, when I "take the field," I want to be ready to …

When God shows up ...
perseverance perfects peace.

GOD'S GROWTH GAUGES

Despite Tony's interception, Woodlawn loses the game against Ensley. As the team enters the locker room, there is total silence, until Coach Gerelds yells out, "How many quarters are there?" … "How many!?" "Four!" a few players call out. Gerelds, fuming, states, "Yeah, four! Not three. Not three and a half!" He emphasizes the last word by knocking over a trashcan. "You blew it! You gave up or wore out. I'm not sure which, but believe me, I am gonna run you into the ground until you can play a complete game of football. Do you understand me?!"

After a pause to look around the locker room, he continues, "Nathan, if you had the courage to stay on the field you mighta' scored! Who is gonna step up on this team? Who is gonna show me what courage and leadership look like?!" Total silence. Gerelds storms out, blowing by Hank in frustration.

Mike Allyson looks at the chaplain and asks, "Hey preacher, I thought you said God was gonna bless us! Thought we were gonna win?" Hank, allowing for the new believer's immaturity, responds, "Well, maybe God is testing us. Maybe He wants to know if our commitment is real and not just to win football games." Allyson has no response, but sitting a few feet away, Tony takes in every word.

God will bless you, if you don't give up when your faith is being tested. He will reward you with a glorious life, just as he rewards everyone who loves him (James 1:12 CEV).

Here are a few specific commands about being in a relationship with God:

Seek the kingdom of God above all else. (Matthew 6:33 NLT)

To be Christ's disciple, you must take up your cross. (Luke 9:23)

Be thankful in all circumstances, for this is God's will. (1 Thessalonians 5:18)

Store up for yourselves treasures in heaven. (Matthew 6:20)

Forgive as your Father has forgiven you. (Colossians 3:13)

Listen to His words and obey. (Matthew 7:24–25)

Tell others that you belong to God. (Matthew 10:32)

Take a few minutes and write out your thoughts about the following open-ended sentences in your journal. Use an abbreviation or a code if you are concerned someone might see what you write.

The one sin with which I have struggled to let go of the most is …

The one area where I have struggled the most to believe God is …

My toughest area to follow God and obey is …

Here are a few maturity markers to encourage and help you gauge your growth:

1. The length of time between your sin and your confession. When we are immature believers, we either aren't convicted by a sin or we are running from God when we do. As you mature, you realize God invites you to confess and get it right immediately—no need for guilt or shame or running away. Maturity leads to quick conviction and fast confession. 1 John 1:9 promises God will always be faithful to forgive.

2. Realizing you no longer have anything to prove—to God or man. Receiving our identity in Christ and making Him our foundation frees us up to stop trying to prove ourselves or please anyone to be approved. God accepts us in Christ, so we accept ourselves, and allow people to choose, as they will, because you are approved in, and by, Him, no matter what anyone thinks.

3. We don't have to be placed into desperate circumstances to realize our dependence on God. God can eventually let up on the level and frequency of testing when we realize and place our full dependence on Him always, even in seasons of great blessing. Desperation for God doesn't have to depend on circumstances, but on commitment.

In your journal today, take a moment and evaluate how you are doing in each of these three areas, then write out a prayer asking God to continue to grow and mature you into His likeness.

SPIRIT SPEAK

On this particular morning, Tony decides to skip his usual run and take the bus to school. He steps on and walks past other African American students to an empty seat near the back. He sees Johnnie, a girl he has noticed several times now at school and at the football games. She is sitting alone. Reggie, one of Tony's buddies who knows he likes her, looks back and motions for him to move up and sit across from her. He quietly gets up and takes the suggestion.

"Hey Johnnie, this is Tony. He don't talk much," Reggie says. Tony just smiles awkwardly. Johnnie pops back, "I know who you are." "Really?" Tony responds, trying to be cool. "Yeah, if you'd scored, we would-a won the game. Why are you so afraid of getting hit?" she challenges with a tone of frustration. " 'Cause it hurts," Tony answers honestly. Johnnie's boldness grows, "Well, too bad."

After an awkward pause from his answer, Johnnie changes the subject back to Reggie's introduction. "So whatcha mean you don't talk much? Why? Is it 'cause you don't have anything to say or because you just too afraid to say it?" Reggie quietly answers, "Both." Johnnie responds, "Reggie, let him talk." "So what's your problem, Tony?" she persists. He pauses to gather his thoughts, then answers, "I don't talk because I like to listen."

God could have made us all into robots with the same

personality and looks. But He didn't. We are all as unique as snowflakes—no two alike. While man has neatly divided personalities into two types—introverts and extroverts—the truth is we all fall on a large sliding scale inside those all-encompassing categories. Right now, as you think about the many people to whom you are close, you can easily see the great diversity and distinction amongst them all.

For the Christian, our personality should not be the driving force behind our lives and our speech. Christ alone should be the gatekeeper of our mouths, who we are, and who we are becoming. His Spirit at work inside an extrovert can teach him/her to be quiet at the proper times and listen, while an introvert can be given the words and the boldness to speak up when prompted.

Christ becomes the overflow of our lives, not our own flesh. We can each look and act like Jesus in our behavior, while still maintaining our unique personality that He placed in us.

Consider these verses from Proverbs:

Thoughtless words can wound as deeply as any sword, but wisely spoken words can heal (12:18 GNT).

As a tree gives fruit, healing words give life, but dishonest words crush the spirit (15:4 NCV).

The heart of the wise has power over his mouth and adds learning to his lips (16:23 NLV).

Tony and Johnnie's interaction is a great example of how different personality types can view each other, as well as misunderstand each other. But, quite often, the vast differences can create a unique attraction of one who is opposite.

Today, connect the dot between your personality and your Christian walk, the connection between your speech and your spirit. Is Christ controlling your mouth? Your attitude? Your actions? We're all a work in progress, but we must constantly be certain we are cooperating with God as He works on that progression!

In your journal:

- Take a moment to write down your own personality type—introvert or extrovert.

- Next, on a scale of one (lowest) to ten (highest), rate the intensity of your personality.

- Write down what you feel is your most dramatic change since becoming a Christian.

- How has this change impacted your personality and speech?

- Write down one prayer you have for God in asking for His help to constantly grow your speech or actions.

When God shows up ...
            hearts can heal.

DISCOVER DIVINE DESTINY

Tony is sitting alone on the bleachers in the gym after practice. Hank enters, walks over to him, and asks, "Hey, Tony. You hear about the bonfire tonight? Can I count you in?" Tony ignores the question and, instead, motions to Hank's leg, "What happened?" "Oh, in college I worked summers at a steel mill. Accident took half my foot and my dreams of pro baseball with it. Man, baseball was everything to me." Tony, not sure what to say, just mutters, "I'm sorry about that." "Don't be," Hank assures. "I think that sometimes before you can have new dreams in this life, the old ones have to be taken away from you."

Hank continues, "Tony, I have something I've wanted to say to you since the first time I saw you play. There's something special about you. I can see it—a gift—something that can't be taught. It can only be given. And you have to decide what to do with it. Now, when you play for yourself, you can be great. But when you play for Something higher than yourself, that's when extraordinary things can happen. God has a purpose for all of us. I can't know, of course, what yours is, but I think God wants you to be a superstar."

Tony just laughs and says, "Ain't no such thing." "As what?" Hank inquires. Showing frustration, Tony finally finds his words, "A black superstar. Not in this state at least. I play on a team that doesn't want me or anyone like me." Hank stands up and says, "We all have a purpose in this life, Tony. I believe God made *you* to run."

Moses was minding his own business, tending to his father-in-law's sheep herd. Suddenly he sees a large bush, totally engulfed in flames, yet it wasn't being consumed. Moses was fascinated. As he draws near, God speaks from the bush, "Moses! Moses!" He answers, "Here I am." After some dialogue, we see God reveal the assignment.

> "Now go, for I am sending you to Pharaoh. You must lead my people Israel out of Egypt." But Moses protested to God, "Who am I to appear before Pharaoh? Who am I to lead the people of Israel out of Egypt?" God answered, "I will be with you. And this is your sign that I am the one who has sent you: When you have brought the people out of Egypt, you will worship God at this very mountain." But Moses protested, "If I go to the people of Israel and tell them, 'The God of your ancestors has sent me to you,' they will ask me, 'What is his name?' Then what should I tell them?" God replied to Moses, "I AM WHO I AM. Say this to the people of Israel: I AM has sent me to you" (Exodus 3:10–14 NLT).

Moses expressed fear, insecurity, self-doubt, and disbelief—even though God's voice was coming from a burning bush. But you know what? We would do the same exact thing, wouldn't we? Why? Because we respond this same way to God all the time.

When Hank was trying to inspire and challenge Tony, he acknowledged his athletic skill but the bigger focus was on God and His plan. Yet rather than hear about God, Tony immediately mentioned the roadblocks in the way. He talked about what he saw and experienced every day, not what God might have for his future.

Moses, like Tony, looked at the roadblocks, not God.

Regardless of where you come from, your background, circumstances, or history, God created you with a clear plan in mind. No matter how you have followed His plan so far, right now, you can make the decision to express faith, instead of what you have seen—or haven't seen. You can take your eyes off your situation and put them on the Savior. God wants to intervene and work in your life just as He did with Moses and Tony.

What is God's plan for you? What roadblocks do you need cleared to move on and discover your divine destiny?

In your journal today, write down:

- What you feel are your greatest roadblocks to achieving all God has for you.

- An action step you can take this week to clear at least one of these roadblocks from your life.

- A prayer asking God to reveal His plan and show His power in your life.

When God shows up ...
truth triumphs.

THE FAITH FACTOR

As Coach Gerelds gets home and goes into his son, Todd's, bedroom to tuck him in, he sees the boy is troubled, and asks, "You okay, Buddy?" Todd answers, "I just hate to lose, Dad. I hate it. Hate it so bad." "Me too," he agrees. "You lied to me, Dad. You say you'll do anything to win, but you won't. … Didn't you see him run?" Todd asks, obviously talking about Tony.

His son's honest and candid words strike Tandy straight to the heart. He knows Todd is right. Out of the mouths of babes, as they say.

In Judges 6, God calls Gideon to leadership. The unassuming farmer has a difficult time wrapping his head around the concept. He decides to be extra sure by asking some quite interesting things of the Almighty.

Gideon said to God, "If you will save Israel by my hand as you have promised—look, I will place a wool fleece on the threshing floor. If there is dew only on the fleece and all the ground is dry, then I will know that you will save Israel by my hand, as you said." And that is what happened. Gideon rose early the next day; he squeezed the fleece and wrung out the dew—a bowlful of water. Then Gideon said to God, "Do not be angry with me. Let me make just one more request. Allow me one more test with the fleece, but this time make the fleece dry and let the ground be covered with dew." That night God did so. Only the fleece was dry; all the ground was covered with dew (Judges 6:36–40 NIV).

As difficult as it may be, try to imagine this scenario from God's perspective. It would be either comical or offensive—or both. But we can all relate, can we not?

There are times in all our lives God will be extremely gracious and patient to allow us to put Him through these ridiculous paces, but, there are also times when He has proven Himself over and over and needs us to just get on board with the plan. Why do you think there are differences in these circumstances? Here are two possibilities to consider:

1. There are times God makes the situation about you and your maturity. When there is a new truth for you to grasp or a new place of growth, God takes the time and effort to lead you at your pace into the Truth. Being our heavenly Father, He sees what you need and wants to provide for your character, as well as your needs.

2. There are times God makes the situation about others. Once you have been trained and prepared for an assignment, God will speak and wants you to respond in obedience for the sake of others. Someone in your circles of influence has a need and God knows you can help. At some point in the past, he has lovingly and patiently trained you for this moment.

In those times, God speaks and wants our …

… compliance, not complaints.

… quest for service, not questions of selfishness.

… expression of faith, not excuses of possible failure.

Coach Gerelds was entering into his own faith journey. God was beginning to speak and work all around him. There is always a point when this begins to take place around you where "figuring it out" can only go so far and faith has to take over. Just like with Gideon.

Your life is the same way. While God will lovingly and patiently work *on* you and *in* you, His ultimate desire is to work *through* you—to change the world.

Complete these sentences in your journal:

The area or place in my life where I feel God is patiently training me is …

The area or place in my life where I feel He is telling me to take action is …

Heavenly Father, I need to stop making excuses and start expressing faith in the area of …

THE FIRE OF FAITH

Just off the south end zone of the football field, a bonfire is burning. The team begins to gather around. Hank looks over the group, then begins to share, "I believe Christianity and football both require sacrifice. Things you have to give up and leave behind. Anything that takes you away from total commitment."

Hank then unfolds a large piece of paper with a black swastika and the words "White Power" written above the symbol, as he states, "I found this behind the gym. Jesus and what is written on this paper cannot coexist. Birmingham has seen nothing but hate for so long that it's lost its ability to believe. It's lost hope. We need someone to show us what it means to live without this. Remember what I said the first time I talked to you in the gym?" One of the players answers, "You told us you loved us." Hank continues, "That's right. And now it's time for you to love each other."

Here's another story that involved a group of strong, young men, a fire, and an incredible display of spiritual commitment in the face of great opposition.

King Nebuchadnezzar had made an image of gold. He ordered that whenever the people heard the music play, they were to fall down and worship the idol. Anyone who refused would be thrown into a blazing fire. Some of the king's advisors came to him and said that three Jewish men—Shadrach,

Meshach, and Abednego—would not bow and serve the idol. Furious and enraged, he brought the three before him and gave them the ultimatum—bow or burn. Their response?

> Shadrach, Meshach and Abednego replied to him, "King Nebuchadnezzar, we do not need to defend ourselves before you in this matter. If we are thrown into the blazing furnace, the God we serve is able to deliver us from it, and he will deliver us from Your Majesty's hand. But even if he does not, we want you to know, Your Majesty, that we will not serve your gods or worship the image of gold you have set up" (Daniel 3:16–18 NIV).

The king's guards threw the men in, but then the king got to see a miracle firsthand. He said, "Look! I see four men walking around in the fire, unbound and unharmed, and the fourth looks like a son of the gods" (verse 25). The king called them out of the flames, saw they were completely unharmed, acknowledged God's rescue, and promoted all three of them!

God's power is best seen through the commitment of His people. Ordinary folks associated with supernatural events. There was no physical explanation for three Jewish men not burning up after being thrown in a raging fire. There would also be no physical explanation for a racially mixed football team in Birmingham, Alabama, in the 1970s, committing to love one another and unite.

As we see the commitment of those in Scripture and as we watch Tony's journey with God unfold, don't miss the very real fact that your heavenly Father wants to do just as big of a work in your life. He loves you. He wants you to help Him change some people's lives. He may never ask you to walk into a fire or take a stand against an evil like racism, but He will ask you to make the same authentic commitment all of these men did. Are you ready? God certainly is!

In your journal today, write down:

- a skill God has given you that you feel He could use for His glory.

- a gift God has given you that you feel He could use for His glory.

- a talent God has given you that you feel He could use for His glory.

Give all these to Him today. Commit them to Him to use as He sees fit, then pray for the opportunities to serve Him with each one.

When God shows up ...
        hearts have hope.

CONFIDENCE
IS A CONTACT SPORT

The game is Woodlawn vs. Hayes with the score in the opposing team's favor. Gerelds turns and looks up into the stands at his son, Todd, who is staring right at him, nodding as if to tell his dad what it is now time to do. The coach calls time out. "Nathan!" he yells out. The offense comes off the field and huddles around.

Gerelds says, "Nathan's in at tailback." Morton protests, "Coach, he don't even know the offense yet, and there's a scout here to see me. A friend of my dad." "Morton!" the coach snaps. "*My* team. Not a democracy." Morton eyes Tony and brushes past him. Tony nervously enters the huddle. Allyson puts out his hand, welcoming him. The coach continues, "Bring it in," as he glances up at his son again. "Power I, guys. Eleven yards. That's what I need. Go get it!"

Gerelds grabs Tony, "You know what I believe. You're faster than them. Show me!" Tony lines up, eyeing the first down marker on the sideline. The ball is snapped. Tony takes the hand off and breaks away, leaping over a linebacker. Hemmed in, he goes out of bounds just past the marker. First down!

As Tony runs back toward the field, Gerelds stops him again, "Nathan! This is a contact sport, okay? When someone wants to hit you, it feels good to hit him first. Try it!" Tony nods, lines up, and starts to calm down. Next play, Hayes blitzes with four men rushing the backfield. Tony's lightning speed wins out, as they all miss. He runs straight for the linebacker and—boom—he runs right into him, carrying him a full five yards before he's brought to the ground. Another first down!

As Tony gets up, something connects inside him. Now, the end zone is just twenty yards away.

We can all relate to Tony's self-doubt and also avoiding opposition rather than hitting it head-on. While there are countless books, talks, and online posts available today about believing in ourselves and being successful, we all struggle with self-image, self-doubt, and personal belief on some level. While gaining confidence is certainly necessary and developing a healthy self-esteem is a positive quality, for the Christian, our God-concept is much more crucial to achieving our purpose in life.

Do you believe God deeply loves you and will forgive you no matter what you do? Or do you believe He really doesn't like you and is constantly disappointed with your failures? Do you believe He provides you with a fresh supply of grace and mercy every morning? Or do you feel as if He says, "Oh, it's you again!"

Try for a moment to erase your ideas about God. Go into your brain and delete the files that are constantly on your screen about Him. Start back at square one.

> But God showed his great love for us by sending Christ to die for us while we were still sinners. And since we have been made right in God's sight by the blood of Christ, he will certainly save us from God's condemnation. For since our friendship with God was restored by the death of his Son while we were still his enemies, we will certainly be saved through the life of his Son. So now

we can rejoice in our wonderful new relationship with God because our Lord Jesus Christ has made us friends of God (Romans 5:8–11 NLT).

If you are a Christian, this passage is all about you! If you are not a Christian, these words are available to you. The choice is yours. God deeply, passionately loves you! The first question to answer is: do you love Him back? God believes in you. The second question to answer is do you believe in Him?

In your journal:

- Write down one negative feeling you tend to have about God.

- How do you feel this impacts your own life and relationship with Him?

- Looking back at Romans 5:8–11, write down the one truth you most need to let sink deep into your soul.

- In your prayer time, confess any struggles or doubts you have with God. He already knows them, so just be honest with your heavenly Father.

When God shows up ...
        souls shine.

THE REACH
OF SPEECH

Celebrating their first win of the season, with a large crowd of family and friends waiting and cheering, the team leaves the locker room. Tony, trying to stay under the radar, comes out to see Johnnie is waiting on him.

She smiles and says, "You looked good out there." Tony grins, thinking this is the best part of the night for him. As they stare into each other's eyes, this is another step closer in their newfound relationship.

Tony's parents walk up to congratulate him. Momma Nathan kisses Tony on the cheek. "Uh … this is Johnnie," Tony says, nervous about Momma Nathan's next move. She looks at Johnnie and says, "She sure is pretty, Tony." He tries to explain, "It's not what you …" But Momma interrupts, "What church you go to? Any woman might marry my son needs to be church goin'."

Tony gives his dad a look. But Johnnie answers, "I don't … go to church." "Well, then you come to church with us. I will fatten you up with my cookin'. How you gonna have a grandbaby with hips like that?" Tony just puts his hands over his face with one of those "Why me, Lord?" expressions. But it's too late—Johnnie is intrigued by his family.

Tony feared what his mom would say, because he was very familiar with her words and how she used them. In this instance, though, Momma would end up getting Johnnie closer to him, into the church, and with his family. He might not have approved of her method, but the result was a win for him.

For us all, words can be a great blessing and a horrible curse. We love what some people say and we cringe at what others utter. Some people are known for speaking wisdom and encouragement, while others are known for unkindness and cruelty. The Bible has much to say about how we speak, where we speak, when we speak, and to whom we speak.

Here are three simple ways to improve what we express to others and some helpful verses for consideration:

1. In the morning, pray for the Holy Spirit to take over your tongue for the entire day. (For most of us, it's usually a good idea to pray again around midday.) "Rather than using clever and persuasive speeches, I relied only on the power of the Holy Spirit" (1 Corinthians 2:4b NLT).

2. Allow a moment to think before speaking. Give God an opportunity to give you the right words. "The heart of the godly thinks carefully before speaking" (Proverbs 15:28a NLT).

3. In a conversation, focus on the other person (or persons) first, not you or your agenda. "Let people finish speaking before you try to answer them" (Proverbs 18:13a ERV).

Tony, who we've already seen is a man of few words, is caught between two ladies who have no trouble speaking their minds. Seems like Momma Nathan and Johnnie are going to get along just fine. But as we will see, God can use Tony to lead with both actions and words.

Is there anyone in your life who fears what you will say? Or maybe more what you *won't* say?

Is there someone close to you whose words bless you consistently, while someone else's words tends to be a curse to you?

You will never be able to control what others say, but you are responsible for your own words and the trail they leave. How much control does the Holy Spirit have over your tongue? The closer you get to Jesus, the more your heart aligns with His; the more your words will reflect His life and love.

In your journal today, complete these prayers:

Lord Jesus, the person whose words I struggle with the most is …

Lord Jesus, the person whose words I am the most blessed by is …

Father, help me today to give You total control of my mouth by …

When God shows up ...
right overrides wrong.

LIVING ON
THE FAULT LINE

After the game, Coach Gerelds is walking out of the locker room to his car when Mike Morton's dad, known to everyone as Bull, walks up. "Tandy." The coach stops. "I've always been straight with you, as you have with me. I want my boy to play college ball. He has that opportunity and it's not fair that it's being taken from him by someone who don't belong."

Gerelds interjects, "I coach the team I am given, Bull. And I coach to win. That is my commitment to myself, this school, and every parent, including you." He starts walking again. Bull pushes Gerelds and gets stronger, "I stayed, Tandy. Lotta people didn't." Gerelds abruptly stops in his tracks. Bull keeps on, "I stayed because you asked me to. I gave you my loyalty and I expect yours in return."

Gerelds stares Bull down, realizing he can't even celebrate a win without another fire being started, as he just turns and walks away. Bull calls out behind him, "Tandy! You're gonna get that colored boy hurt." The coach just keeps going.

Favors. Promises. Expectations. Intentions. Trust. Understanding. Misunderstanding. Deals—both contracts and handshakes. Conflict arises every day based on these concepts. What people mean by what they say is quite often different than what is heard and interpreted. People forget what they agreed to or don't recall a conversation the same way as the other person.

Juries meet every day to listen to and decide upon who was in the right and who was in the wrong, and—where the truth is in a situation.

Where does the fault lie in most situations? Ninety-nine percent of the time the blame is shared between both parties. Sure, the ratio might be 10 percent fault for one person and 90 percent to the other, but even still, each person must own up to his share.

Perspective is the way we view a situation. Perception is how we process what we see.

Consider this scenario … five people witness a crime. Ask any law enforcement officer and they will tell you in the vast majority of cases, five witnesses means five different stories and five different perceptions.

Think about interviewing people as they leave a movie. Does everyone like the movie? Of course not. Some will, some won't. Ask those people to tell you the plot and you will hear slightly different versions, based on their own perceptions.

There is an old saying that goes, "Perception is reality." This simply means what someone believes they see is real to that person.

As Christians, the more faith we apply to our perspective, the more our perception of God's activity in the world will grow. The more of God we allow in, the more of God we can then see. This is why you cannot talk anyone into becoming a Christ follower. Faith has to change a person's perspective and perception.

On this side of heaven, it is impossible to rid our lives of all conflict and misunderstanding. But, as we grow in Christ, we can maximize our own perspective and perception to view people and circumstances as Christ would, while allowing love and grace for those with which we communicate.

> So if you're serious about living this new resurrection life with Christ, act like it. Pursue the things over which Christ presides. Don't shuffle along, eyes to the ground, absorbed with the things right in front of you. Look up, and be alert to what is going on around Christ—that's where the action is. See things from *his* perspective (Colossians 3:1–2 MSG).

How big is God in your reality? Is He included in your own perspective of the world? Does He impact your perception of people?

Just like we see Coach Gerelds constantly dealing with conflict from all sides, our lives are often equally as challenging. A continual surrendering to Christ will bring a greater wisdom and ability to "see things from *his* perspective."

In your journal today, prayerfully complete these action points:

- Write down your biggest conflict right now.

- Write down your most recent misunderstanding with someone.

- Based on these situations, what can you learn and what did God show you in how these were handled?

- List one thing you can do today to change your perspective to how you believe Jesus would have you view those around you.

RISE UP & RUN STRONG

Sunday-morning light pours in through the stained glass windows at St. James Baptist Church, a small but close fellowship. The preacher is pacing about the pulpit, fueled in his message by frequent "amen's" from the members. He shares, "Therefore, seeing we are surrounded by such a great cloud of witnesses, let us lay aside every weight and the sin that does so easily beset us, and let us run with patience the race set before us."

Tony is struggling to pay attention. Today, he's more focused on the back door than the platform, because Johnnie has yet to show. Suddenly, he smiles, as she quietly slips in to sit with the Nathan's. Tony's mom nudges his dad, grins, and calls out, "Amen and amen!"

The pastor is just getting started as he declares, "Who's got a race they need to run today? Who needs to rise up? We need those who will accomplish what God has laid before them. We need someone who can endure suffering because they are looking to Jesus—to the cross, to a new day, to a better day. So I say to you, 'Rise up. Rise up!' Somebody's gotta rise up!"

Tony lets the challenge sink in. Johnnie's eyes are fixed on him. Something special is happening here; they just can't quite make out exactly what it is yet.

Let's take a deeper look at the passage from which the pastor quoted—Hebrews 12:1–3:

> We are surrounded by a great cloud of people whose lives tell us what faith means. So let us run the race that is before us and never give up. We should remove from our lives anything that would get in the way and the sin that so easily holds us back. Let us look only to Jesus, the One who began our faith and who makes it perfect. He suffered death on the cross. But he accepted the shame as if it were nothing because of the joy that God put before him. And now he is sitting at the right side of God's throne. Think about Jesus' example. He held on while wicked people were doing evil things to him. So do not get tired and stop trying (NCV).

Paul's imagery is that of a sporting event where spectators are seated all around viewing the race; except this is not your normal crowd, for each one has also run their own race. So, because of this heavenly company cheering us on, let's look at four truths available to us.

1. Run your race. God has given you a specific lane to run in, at a specific time in history. Be faithful to run hard and fast right where He has placed you.

2. Never give up. Every runner or athlete knows that moment when you run out of strength, get injured, or feel like you will pass out if you don't stop. In those moments, you must look to and receive Christ's strength to keep going. After all, like Tony, our race is never just about us, but others who are counting on us to be faithful and finish.

3. Get rid of excess baggage. Sin can hinder and even end our race. Paul puts the responsibility of handing over our issues squarely on us. We can choose to rid ourselves of them, just as we chose to take them up. Christ offers forgiveness, grace, and deliverance for everything that slows us down.

4. Look only at Jesus. Runners who look to the side or even back to see where others are positioned often lose focus, then the race. While Jesus gives us strength to run, He is also the One standing at the finish line. Fixing our eyes on Him as the ultimate Goal keeps us running to win.

Jesus took on His assignment for God, stayed true to His mission, and only sought to please His Father. Tony was about to embark on his mission, carrying far more than a football to the goal line.

What about you? What race are you running? Is there anything hindering you? How can you focus more on Jesus to win?

Today, you can rise up and run your race!

In your journal, list the one thing ...

- that most causes you to want to give up.
- in your life you know you need to get rid of.
- you know you could do to inspire you to follow Jesus in a deeper way.

When God shows up ...
    faith fractures fear.

CALLED & COURAGEOUS

Coach Gerelds and Coach Stearns are having dinner at a local diner. After the waitress brings their food, Stearns bows his head and silently prays. Gerelds is immediately uncomfortable. He then asks Stearns, "So you're all in, huh?" referring to his newfound faith he shares with the team. Stearns nods his head.

Just then, Shorty White, the head coach of Banks High and Woodlawn's archrival, walks in with another coach. He's long been the most successful coach in the city.

Shorty looks over to Gerelds across the diner and yells, "We're a-comin' for you, Tandy. Eight more weeks to Judgment Day, boy. Glorious rivalry day. Banks' Jets is comin' for you in the clouds. I'm bringin' my white knight. Maybe you heard about him? Jeff Rutledge. The best quarterback in the state. I'm just quotin' the *Birmingham News*. They printed that."

Gerelds starts to sarcastically applaud the speech. The words hit Gerelds like a bucket of ice water, while the righteous anger rises up in his gut. This is what it must feel like to be on the receiving end of ignorance.

Faith in Christ is not for cowards, but the courageous. Turning the other cheek is not weakness; it's strength. Anger doesn't need to be displayed when pity is actually the more proper response.

Check out this passage in Proverbs:

Simpletons! How long will you wallow in ignorance? Cynics! How long will you feed your cynicism? Idiots! How long will you refuse to learn? About face! I can revise your life. Look, I'm ready to pour out my spirit on you; I'm ready to tell you all I know. As it is, I've called, but you've turned a deaf ear; I've reached out to you, but you've ignored me (1:22–24 MSG).

The writer is speaking under divine inspiration from God's perspective. Notice that even though the language is quite strong in the first few sentences, there is an offer from God contained in the words. Let's take a closer look.

1. Response. "As it is, I've called." When we walk away and wander into the darkness, God responds by calling out, letting us know where He is, and telling us where we should be. In this passage, God says, "You've turned a deaf ear." Just as we can decide to not listen, we can also decide to tune in and obey.

2. Reach. "I've reached out to you." God is proactive, always reaching to rescue, restore, and redeem. When we answer God's call, we can become His hands and feet, cross the dividing lines, borders, and bridges to show people His love is available to all.

3. Righteousness. "Look, I'm ready to pour out my spirit on you." The world's way of living right is constantly changing. As sin becomes accepted, the standards keep moving. God's brand of right living—righteousness—is only possible and available through His Spirit. He is ready to give us all we need to live as He created us to live.

4. Relationship. "I'm ready to tell you all I know." God is making His mind and heart available to us. He wants to be integrally involved in and with His people—with you.

Every day, we see and hear accounts of rampant hate and prejudice, just like what was reflected in the coaches' conversation. True revival can come when we realize these four "R" elements are stronger than any other force in our world.

In your journal, write down:

- a few sentences of how you believe God has called you to Himself.

- how God reached out to you.

- one example of how God has poured out His Spirit on you.

- one way your relationship with God can be the catalyst to bring revival to those around you.

When God shows up ...
    the miraculous materializes.

ON THIS DAY!

The Huffman Eagles are the number one team in the state of Alabama. They have beaten every opponent by an average of twenty-eight points with no one scoring on them. Because of these stats, no one believes Woodlawn even has a chance to win.

In the locker room, Coach Gerelds tells the team, "Okay, boys, listen up. The preacher wants to say a few words." He then looks at Hank and says, "Make it good."

Hank walks over and asks Tony to read a Bible passage. Tony reads the verses and Hank then finishes the story of David and Goliath. Hank keeps going. "You're going to win this game tonight. You hear me? You're going to win this game. You know how I know you're going to win this game? Because it's not about you. Nobody out there knows what is happening on this team. But when you win on this day, they will. When you do what everyone said is impossible, they will. When you strike down this giant, they will. And when they find out how you did it, then all the earth will know there is a God in Israel!" Then Hank begins to chant, "On this day! On this day!" as the team begins to join him.

Coach Gerelds, uncertain of what to make of this speech, walks over to Tony and says, "Nathan, you're starting at tailback tonight."

Moments later Gerelds walks into the bathroom to find

Tony nervously writing on some tape on the back of his helmet. The two walk together out onto the field.

Huffman quickly scores and Mike Allyson shuffles to the sideline and tells Gerelds, "They're big, coach. Really big." The crowd prepares for a massacre.

Hank walks over to Tony as he waits to go in and says, "What do you say you go in there right now and take down that giant? Make them believe." Tony takes the field, his first start as tailback. On the very first handoff, he breaks free and scores. As he turns in the end zone, we see the message on his helmet: "Believe. No Fear." In every quarter, he dominates the running game and Woodlawn, miraculously, wins. His new nickname is born: "Touchdown" Tony Nathan.

> David said to the Philistine, "You come against me with sword and spear and javelin, but I come against you in the name of the Lord Almighty, the God of the armies of Israel, whom you have defied. This day the Lord will deliver you into my hands, and I'll strike you down … and the whole world will know that there is a God in Israel" (1 Samuel 17:45–46 NIV).

Let's look at three key points of David's faithfulness, before and during his victory.

1. David was faithful to his assignment. His dad had placed him in the field, often alone, tending to the sheep. But then changed his assignment to taking food to his brothers on the battlefield. Of course, God was actually Who was assigning David to each task. Training as a shepherd and time alone with God prepared him for what was to come as warrior and king.

2. David was faithful to his authority. He had done what his dad asked him to do and now was submitting to the king. Life was about to go from very private to quite public. Understanding the flow chart of authority from God is crucial to being at the right place at the right time.

3. David was faithful to the assault. An assault is an offensive military attack. From David's words to his final defeat of the enemy, he carried out exactly what had to be done and what he said he would do. He was never in a defensive position in this account, because he stayed on the offense by faith.

There is great opportunity and great blessing to be found when we are faithful to God's assignment, authority, and assault.

In your journal, answer these questions:

- What assignments from God are you currently carrying out?

- Where are you submitting to authority and where are you struggling?

- What are steps you can take to get off the defensive and be "faithful to the assault"—being proactive for the Lord?

When God shows up ...
heaven inhabits hearts.

NEW DAY, NEW LIFE

Woodlawn defeats Huffman! The entire home crowd, black and white together, rushes out onto the field. Johnnie runs into Tony's arms and they kiss. This is the greatest moment of his young life with so many roads intersecting all at once.

In the chaos amidst the rush and push of all the people, the coach of Huffman finds Gerelds at midfield. "Great game, Coach," he says, shaking Tandy's hand. "I don't know what your players are playing with, but I've never seen a team play like that."

As the Huffman coach walks away, Gerelds looks over at Hank. He smiles and holds up a small stone to remind the coach of the locker room declaration of "On this day!" Something moves deep inside Gerelds' soul. Though surrounded by fans and friends slapping him on the back and congratulating him, he has never felt so alone in his life. Like being lost inside the familiar, his heart is aching for more.

The crowd is long since gone. Hours drift by. As the edge of the sun begins to peer over the horizon and the landscape turns that early morning blue, Gerelds is still there, sitting in the empty bleachers. He's been there all night, searching, questioning his life and who he is. Tandy looks at the new dawn as tears stream down his face. Finally, in a quiet whisper, he prays, "God, I don't know if You're real, but I want whatever my players have." All the pent-up emotion starts pouring out from months of trying to manage so many impossible circumstances.

Coach Tandy Gerelds gave up his life to find it—into the arms of a loving Savior, Who was waiting patiently for him.

From the moment Hank Erwin knocked on the coach's door, God was coming after Tandy. He was pursuing him with His great love and grace. Every situation that created problems and pressure brought him another step closer to Jesus. Tony's phrase on his helmet had become a call to a new mindset and motivation for living.

"The Son of Man came to seek and to save the lost" (Luke 19:10 GNT).

Jesus makes it abundantly clear in this single, powerful verse that it is He Who seeks out the lost and then offers salvation, just as He did with Tandy and the team. Through the soul searching of that long night at the football stadium, Jesus alone met the coach on his own turf, quite literally, and brought him home.

Throughout the centuries, people have attempted to attach other actions to salvation. The truth of Scripture is clear that adding anything to Jesus, making it a necessity for redemption, is a false claim. Christ alone saves. Good works don't save us. A certain church won't save us. A life of being a "good" person won't save. God's Spirit draws us and we can then respond in faith.

We sometimes hear folks say, "I found Jesus!" While we may understand what they are attempting to express, we do not find Him. He is not lost; we are! We do nothing to receive salvation except to express faith in Him. We then respond to His free gift by submitting in obedience to Him.

A Christ follower is saved by grace—unmerited favor—and through that gift is able to join the heavenly Father in His kingdom work until heaven.

Anytime we, or anyone, attempts to attach anything to Christ for salvation, it is unbiblical and not of the Truth. So, it is Jesus = salvation, never Jesus + x = salvation. Our obedience and actions are simply a response to His great gift of love.

Because Jesus is seeking to save the lost and He will do the saving, we must always be mindful to be in His will, while staying out of His way. This simply means we make ourselves available to those whom He is touching, reaching, and calling, while not rushing in to try and do the saving.

Do you see God working to seek someone around you in your circles of influence right now?

Can you sense Him drawing someone you know?

How can you help the person in their move toward faith?

In your journal, take a moment to write down your answers to the questions above and how you can be more accepting, attentive, and available to what Jesus is doing in the lives of those around you.

OF BLOOD & WATER

At Tony's church, the pastor is well into his message. To everyone's surprise, the back doors of the church open and a hush falls over the congregation. Coach Gerelds and his family walk in. They are obviously the only white people in the church. They quietly walk toward the front.

The coach asks, "Can I say a few words, please sir?" The pastor responds, "Okay. Come on then!" Gerelds faces the crowd and, more humble than anyone has ever seen him before, says, "I wanted to come here today because five of my players are here; five of my players that have been mistreated time and again by their school and by their teammates … and I have not done enough to stop it. At the beginning of the season, my team, nearly my entire team, gave themselves to Christ. They surrendered to Love—a love that I didn't understand. A love that began to conquer hatred. I come here today to say that I want whatever my players have. I came here today because I believe." Tandy tears up, as the people respond with "amens" and the pastor shouts.

Gerelds closes with, "I believe and I want to be baptized." The church erupts with applause.

Within a few minutes, the pastor and the coach enter the water together. "I baptize you, my brother, in the name of the Father and the Son and the Holy Spirit. Buried with Christ in baptism, raised to walk in newness of life." Tandy looks out to see his wife, his son, and … Tony.

When Woodlawn was divided by brutal hatred and everyone had chosen sides, who would have ever seen this sacred and miraculous event coming? Only God—and someone with the eyes of faith—a man like Hank Erwin who believed God could change an entire team.

In Matthew chapter 3, we meet John the Baptist. He was preaching in the wilderness of Judea. People were responding to his messages, confessing sin, and being baptized from Jerusalem and the entire region of the Jordan River. Then, one day, prophecy was fulfilled and everything changed.

> Then Jesus came from Galilee to the Jordan to be baptized by John. But John tried to deter him, saying, "I need to be baptized by you, and do you come to me?" Jesus replied, "Let it be so now; it is proper for us to do this to fulfill all righteousness." Then John consented. As soon as Jesus was baptized, he went up out of the water. At that moment heaven was opened, and he saw the Spirit of God descending like a dove and alighting on him. And a voice from heaven said, "This is my Son, whom I love; with him I am well pleased" (Matthew 3:13–17 NIV).

Imagine being given the privilege to baptize Jesus, see the Holy Spirit in the form of a dove, and hear the audible voice of God? Incredible. John had been preaching in faith, believing the Messiah was coming, but not knowing when.

Hank Erwin knew God was going to turn things around at Woodlawn, so he pressed on in faith even when doors closed in his face—literally—and circumstances looked very dire. But, now, the people in the African American church got to see the head football coach walk in, ask for forgiveness, and be baptized. Every move of God is a miracle. But it must start with an expression of faith.

The blood of Christ, shed on the cross for all sin, makes our souls the same color, which is the only thing that matters in the kingdom of God. The common bond of the crimson red blood of Jesus brings us together in His name.

If you are a follower of Christ, have you been baptized? If not, consider following your Lord's example in this amazing experience. If so, write out some of your feelings about that moment in your journal.

In your journal, thinking back to your own baptism, take a few minutes to evaluate your level of faith and excitement during that time in your life.

- Where are you today in your walk with Christ compared to that day?

- Are there any steps you need to take you reengage your faith to return to that place and then move beyond in your spiritual growth? Write down your thoughts.

When God shows up …
holiness heals the home.

THE FATHER'S HEART

Back at home Tandy enters his son's room at night, after the boy is already in bed. "Hey, son. Can we talk a minute?" He snaps up quickly and says, "Sure."

"Son, I know it's been a tough year at school. And I know we haven't seen much of each other." Todd responds, "That's okay, Dad." "No. There's no excuse for it. I love you and you mean the world to me. I think my biggest problem is that I just don't have enough staff, so I was wondering if you'd be willing to help me out ... as an assistant coach?" Todd's eyes go wide and his face lights up like it hasn't in far too long. "I was thinking with the running backs," Tandy says, as he hands a Woodlawn coaching cap to his son.

The very next scene is Todd being dragged in a tire behind Tony with the newest and smallest coach yelling, "You're good, but you're not that good! Pick up those knees!" The team has a new mascot and they love it. While the coaches no longer tend to yell at all, Todd is a little drill sergeant, making up for everyone else. And Tandy and Todd's relationship has never been stronger.

The family was the first entity of God's creation that he ordained—even before the church. There is no question that the Enemy of God hates the family and is out to destroy every one he can. We see this happening all around us every day.

"When God shows up" in a home, priorities always change sooner than later. Why? Certainly we are to place His kingdom first, but in that kingdom, the family is His prized showpiece. Love begins to have full reign. Relationships are valued. Busyness gives way to blessing those in the home.

In the Gospel of Luke, an angel foretells the ministry of John the Baptist to his father. Take a look at what God said his work would accomplish.

> "He will help many people of Israel return to the Lord their God. He will go before the Lord in spirit and power like Elijah. He will make peace between parents and their children and will bring those who are not obeying God back to the right way of thinking, to make a people ready for the coming of the Lord" (Luke 1:16–17 NCV).

John would …

… help God's chosen people to turn to Him.

… make peace between parents and children.

… bring the lost back home to God.

… make God's people ready for the coming of Christ.

Imagine the impact on our culture if families began to get emotionally and spiritually healthy on a large scale. Lives would vastly improve, society would benefit, and God would be glorified. Fathers would sit down beside the beds of their children and get things right. Moms would sit at the kitchen table and hear the hearts of her kids.

Consider your own family for a moment. If God had his way in every life, what would change? How would you change?

What relationship might be made right or, at least, be attempted to be made right, freeing you from any burden or guilt?

Tandy didn't just commit to spend more time with Todd—he involved him deeper into his life and invested into his son's own dreams. This renewed connection then blessed all the other players and coaches, as well as the Gerelds' family.

What investment would God have you make in your family? What blessings is God waiting to deliver? Whose dreams can you help make a reality, through His leadership?

In your journal, write down:

- what you would like to see God do in your own family. Include any extended family if you'd like.

- any steps you could take to bring Christ and His priorities more into focus in your family.

- a family member you might need to talk with soon.

DAY 26

MESSAGE MANIFESTO

Cedric is playing in the den at the front of the house. A car pulls up out front. He goes to the window to see who it is. As he pulls the curtain back, a brick crashes through the glass. Shocked and frightened, the boy is frozen with fear.

He peers through the broken glass to see a man lighting a cross with a football jersey draped over it—numbered with "22"—Tony's.

Momma Nathan runs into the den as the car speeds away. They are both stunned at the sight of the cross on their lawn.

Soon, Tony and Junior enter the house in a rush, still dressed in their best clothes from attending a sports awards banquet. Momma is holding Cedric, who is clutching his blanket, terrified.

Tony sits down beside them. "You okay, Champ?" He just shakes his head, then says, "They gonna hurt you. They gonna hurt me." Big brother assures, "No, they won't. I won't let 'em." "You weren't here, Tony," Cedric responds.

Tony walks over to the shattered window and picks up the brick. A note is attached with a two-word message: "Quit football."

Scared and ignorant people wanted to stop what was happening at Woodlawn. Ironically, the very object the racists set on fire on the Nathan's lawn was the real reason and motivation for what was happening in the community—the cross.

The power of the gospel has been the driving force behind

change in many cultures. And people have always wanted to stop it.

Peter and John and the other apostles were teaching the people about Jesus, His resurrection, and ascension to heaven. The high priests were upset that the message was continuing even after they were certain they had gotten rid of Him. Feeling they needed to quiet them quickly, they threw Peter and John in jail.

The next day, the two were brought before the rulers, elders, and teachers of the Law in Jerusalem. They spoke confidently and boldly to the questions asked of them. In the midst of being warned to stop talking to everyone about Christ, we find two key Scriptures in this passage that are inspiring to us today.

> When they saw the courage of Peter and John and realized that they were unschooled, ordinary men, they were astonished and they took note that these men had been with Jesus (Acts 4:13 NIV).

> "As for us, we cannot help speaking about what we have seen and heard" (Acts 4:20 NIV).

When told to stop preaching the truth of Jesus, Peter and John's response was essentially, "We cannot *not* talk about Him."

They did let them go. And the apostles never stopped talking about Jesus.

If you are a Christ follower today, the reason is because someone decided the message was worth talking about, sharing, and risking—with you. Even in our digital age of media, the vast majority of people who come to Christ still do so through a personal relationship with a believer.

When you prove yourself to the point that Tony had, people

start taking notice. When you prove yourself to the point Peter and John had, people start taking notice. No one could ignore an obvious fact—their words and actions were proving they had a strong relationship with Jesus Christ.

As Christians, our lives will either attract or distract, meaning we will draw people to Him or away from Him. What about you? Which one do you feel your life creates in others?

If the answer is "attract," great! If your answer is "distract," here's some good news. You can turn things around, just like Tony and the team. And consider Peter, who denied Jesus three times at His trial, but is now saying he can't be silenced about his Lord. God specializes in second chances.

In your journal:

- Is there somewhere in your life where you aren't talking about Jesus and should start?

- Is there a place you are creating a distraction from Christ? What can you do to change directions?

- What is one thing you can do to make people aware you "have been with Jesus"?

IF YOU WANT GOD ...

Mike Allyson and Tony walk out to the parking lot after school. A lone figure is leaning against a pickup truck. As they get closer, they realize it's Jeff Rutledge, the star quarterback for Banks High.

Jeff speaks first: "Hey Nathan, you're smaller than you look on TV." Tony quips back, "So are you." Allyson asks, "Jeff Rutledge? Why are you here? Is the rest of Banks here too?" Jeff doesn't answer, prompting Mike to realize and remember a long-held rivalry prank. "Are they paintin' our steps blue?!" Mike asks in a panic. Jeff calmly answers, "Rivalry week." Mike takes off running for the back of the school, calling out, "Heck no! Heck no!" Rutledge yells out behind Mike, "But it's tradition!"

Tony asks, "Why you not with 'em?" "Cause they're morons," the quarterback answers. Tony looks at him, nodding in approval.

Jeff says, "I heard what's happening over here. Wish I could be a part of something like that. I'm a Christian. Banks is a pretty lonely place. Love to hear the story, Tony."

In the days of the early church, the line between Jews and Gentiles was clearly and broadly drawn. But we see a major paradigm shift in Acts 10. Peter had been praying and stopped to eat. He had a vision from God to no longer call anything impure that God has made clean. Following this, the Holy Spirit spoke and told him that three men were looking for him and he should go with them, because God had sent them.

Peter found the men and they told him they had been sent by a man named Cornelius, a centurion. They told Peter he was a God-fearing and righteous man who was widely respected. They said Cornelius had been visited by an angel that told him to have Peter speak to his household.

Peter went to the centurion's home and they shared how God had moved in them both to bring them together. Let's take up the story there.

> Peter fairly exploded with his good news: "It's God's own truth, nothing could be plainer: God plays no favorites! It makes no difference who you are or where you're from—if you want God and are ready to do as he says, the door is open. The Message he sent to the children of Israel—that through Jesus Christ everything is being put together again—well, he's doing it everywhere, among everyone (Acts 10:34–36 MSG).

By seeking out Tony, Jeff not only crossed town and rival school boundary lines, but also the racial boundary. Why? Because the common ground of Christ was his biggest draw, as well as his greatest concern. He wanted to hear Tony's story for himself, just like Cornelius wanted to hear Peter's message.

Jeff Rutledge and Cornelius, the centurion, didn't have a well-traveled road to get to Tony or Peter. These men had to blaze a trail in an area where no path had been cleared before. In this world, there have always been pioneers and settlers. Pioneers are those who will blaze the trail alone in places no one has traveled before. Settlers are those who follow to join them, once the road is proven. The world needs both, yet someone always has to decide to blaze the trail that has yet to be traveled.

Which are you—a pioneer or a settler? In the kingdom of God, which are you?

Does the Lord tend to call you to faith-driven expeditions into new territory? Or does He have you follow in well-worn places of ministry to support? Do you tend to see places where ministry does not exist and have a vision for the details of how to accomplish it? Do you tend to ask for someone to put you to work in a ministry that exists but needs help? Do you see how both are desperately needed roles in the work of God?

Just like today's verse states, "It makes no difference who you are or where you're from—if you want God and are ready to do as he says, the door is open."

In your journal, complete these sentences:

I believe I am a pioneer/settler because …

A place I consistently see God use me is …

A new place of ministry I feel God may want to use me is …

When God shows up …
saints stand strong and steady.

FAITHFUL IN
A FALLEN WORLD

For Tony, life feels like it is going south fast. With the pressures of being the "star player" at Woodlawn, Mike Morton and his gang, and his rocky relationship with Johnnie, he is struggling and hurting. In fact, he would likely want to be anywhere tonight except on the football field, lined up against the rival team with the racist coach, calling out slurs against him.

Coach Gerelds brings the team into the pregame huddle. "Come on, men. Everyone. Let's go. Now." The whole team gathers around him and they hit one knee, bowing their heads, as most all of them recite, "Our Father, who art in heaven, hallowed by Thy name..."

Across the field, Banks' coach, Shorty White, calls out, mocking, "Jesus can't save you now, boys! This is football!"

We hear the sportscaster: "As you know, these two schools are within five miles of each other and that means only one can go to the playoffs. This is the final test for Woodlawn. One they must overcome to survive. Whoever goes home tonight goes home for good."

The team finishes their prayer. "For Thine is the kingdom and the power and the glory forever. Amen." Tony forces himself up from one knee. Gerelds notices Tony's usual spirit and drive are gone and the coach can tell. As Tony trots onto the field, the coach realizes something is not right.

Just living can suck the life out of us, can't it? Bad things happen. People hurt us and let us down. Circumstances don't go our way. Stress can make us feel like invisible weights are pushing us deeper into the ground. We all know very well what discouragement feels like.

God knows how much this broken and fallen world affects us. That is why throughout the Bible one of his most repeated commands is to be strong, have courage, and to not be afraid. Take a look at how Moses repeated the words before Joshua and the people of Israel in Deuteronomy 31:6–8.

> Be strong and brave. Don't be afraid of them and don't be frightened, because the LORD your God will go with you. He will not leave you or forget you." Then Moses called Joshua and said to him in front of the people, "Be strong and brave, because you will lead these people into the land the Lord promised to give their ancestors, and help them take it as their own. The Lord himself will go before you. He will be with you; he will not leave you or forget you. Don't be afraid and don't worry (NCV).

Let's look at this passage, phrase by phrase, for encouragement today.

Be strong.	Be brave.
Don't be afraid.	Don't be frightened.
Your God will go with you.	God will not leave you.
God will not forget you.	Be strong and brave.
The Lord will go before you.	God will be with you.
God will not leave you.	God will not forget you
Don't be afraid.	Don't worry.

While this is God's message to Israel, we can certainly apply these truths to our lives today. His truth never changes. Do you see how when you read these phrases one after another, it sounds much like a loving parent trying to reassure a child that all is well, even though the child may be afraid or upset at the time? Well, that is exactly what is happening—the Father is comforting His children by repeated reassurance.

What difference might it make in your own life, even at this moment, if you not only read these simple statements but truly believed and took them to heart?

We are going to have bad days, rough patches, and difficult seasons. God knows this well, so His constant encouragement in His Word is a message we can emblazon on our minds and hearts to keep us going, to hold our heads up above the floodwaters of life, and to keep pressing on through adversity.

In your journal, write down:

- your biggest struggle in life right now.

- your greatest blessing in life right now.

- the place you most want to see God work to make you brave.

TIME TO CALL
"TIME OUT"

Touchdown Tony, though playing hurt and exhausted in the rain, is barreling down the field, breaking tackles. Just as he slows down crossing the goal line, Coach Shorty White yells, "Take him out! Take … him … out!" A safety runs in full speed and delivers a late hit. Even though the ref throws the flag, the damage has been done. Coach Gerelds storms onto the field, the team angered and protesting.

With help, Tony limps to the sideline and collapses on the bench. The team doctor looks him over, as Tandy stands by, then says, "Coach, you're taking a real risk if you play him." Gerelds kneels down and looks Tony in the eye, "We win with you. We can't win without you. Got it? Adversity is the crucible of greatness, Tony." At that moment, the Jets score again.

As Coach Gerelds watches Tony limp onto the field, he pauses a moment as reality sets in. "Nathan! Time out. Time out!" he calls to the refs. He walks onto the field, grabs Tony, and walks off the field with him. Coach White continues to mock from the opposite sideline about the team's faith.

Back in the locker room at the end of the game, the team is covered in mud and completely dejected. Tony walks out into the hallway. The coach follows him. Angered and crying, Tony screams, "Coach, why didn't you play me?!" Gerelds grabs him, as a strange peace comes over him, and says, "You know what's more important to me than winning football games?" He places his hands on Tony's shoulders and answers, "You are. ... You are." The white coach and the African American athlete embrace as the mutual respect and their newfound brotherhood overcome them both.

In our crazy culture, people would rather look at a five-inch screen than into a person's eyes. Our society is devaluing people and the problem grows worse by the year.

Think about how many people you encounter in a single day. Think about yesterday and everyone you stood in front of and dealt with on any level—the ones you felt that "matter" and the ones who didn't. Think about your spouse, children, employees, bosses, coworkers, friends, clerks, baristas, waiters, and the random person in line beside you.

Consider these questions:

Do you tend to humanize people you encounter? Or do you tend to dehumanize?

Here are some examples of things we can think on a given day:

"I just have to get my kid to school. I don't want to talk or think about what he/she saying. I just need to get to work."

"Lady, I'm just trying to get a cup of coffee from you. Please don't ask me how I'm doing."

"Dude, I don't have time to hear about your problem. What do you need?"

"I don't want to focus on what this person is saying. I've got too many things to do."

Those are dehumanizing attitudes that drive dehumanizing actions. This creates a lack of eye contact, a lack of attention. Distraction. Self-focus. Agendas.

Here are some examples of humanizing people:

"Jesus reached out his hand and touched the man."

"As Jesus went on from there, he saw a man named Matthew sitting at the tax collector's booth."

"Jesus turned and saw her."

"Just then his disciples returned and were surprised to find him talking with a woman."

Jesus humanized people everywhere. He valued them. He cared about them. He took the time to focus, make eye contact, pay attention, and engage.

Today, slow down. Humanize the humans—all of them. Tell them what Coach Gerelds said to Tony. "You know what's more important to me than (fill in the blank) right now? You are." That attitude will change some lives—in Jesus' name.

"Do you love me?" He said, "Lord, you know all things; you know that I love you." Jesus said, "Feed my sheep" (John 21:17 NIV).

Let love be your only debt! If you love others, you have done all that the Law demands (Romans 13:8 CEV).

In your journal:

- Write down the name of at least one person you know you can tend to "dehumanize."

- Beside his/her name, write down one act of love you can offer the next time you see that person.

- List one practical thing you can do to slow down a bit and engage with people.

RISK, REWARD & REASSURANCE

After Sunday church, as the Nathan family drives up to their house, they notice a nice car parked out front and a man standing and waiting. As Tony gets out of the car and walks up, the man says, "Hello, Son. I'm Coach Bryant." Legendary Coach Bear Bryant has come to Tony's home to offer him a spot on his team.

After one of his famous recruiting speeches, Junior asks, "How many black players you have?" The coach answers, "I don't have white players and black players. I just have football players. That's how I see it. ... But to answer your question, not nearly enough." "Why you see that changing?" Tony asks. "Because it's time," Bryant answers with confidence. "Now you gonna help me?"

Tony likes the answer, but looks past Coach Bryant to the window where the brick came through into his home. Feeling the invisible, but very present pressure, Tony quietly gets up and walks out.

Junior steps outside too. "I'm sorry, Dad. I know that was disrespectful." His dad responds, "Ah. Ain't no problem. Your momma's talkin' his ear off anyway." "Football just hurts me and everyone around me," Tony shares. "Nobody's forcing you to play football. You know that, right?" Junior asks. "You can walk away right now and let the world pass on by. But this is bigger than football, ain't it?" Tony responds, "Yes, sir."

Junior says, as only a loving father can, "Some kinda great power has been given to you, son. I've seen the look on those kids' faces. I know what they're thinking, 'A black star like you at a white school. If he can do it, so can I.' That is your gift. This is your time, to do as you choose."

Tony looks at his dad. "So tell me what to do and I'll do it."

Then Jesus went with his disciples to a place called Gethsemane … and he began to be sorrowful and troubled. Then he said to them, "My soul is overwhelmed with sorrow to the point of death. Stay here and keep watch with me." Going a little farther, he fell with his face to the ground and prayed, "My Father, if it is possible, may this cup be taken from me. Yet not as I will, but as you will." Then he returned to his disciples and found them sleeping. … He went away a second time and prayed, "My Father, if it is not possible for this cup to be taken away unless I drink it, may your will be done." When he came back, he again found them sleeping, because their eyes were heavy. So he left them and went away once more and prayed the third time, saying the same thing. Then he returned to the disciples and said to them, "Look, the hour has come … Rise! Let us go!" (Matthew 26:36–46 NIV).

In this life, there will be a handful of crucial, life-changing moments that are critical to our future and those around us. In those moments, we feel the weight of the sacrifice we are being asked to make. We sense the great responsibility of the task we are being called to take on. We realize life on the other side of this decision will likely never be the same.

Tony was facing just such a moment. He could sense it, see it, and feel it deep within him. Jesus faced many of these moments, but none greater or stronger than in the garden of Gethsemane. He knew the cross was right around the corner and the weight of the world was quite literally on His shoulders.

Have you faced a crossroads moment in your life? Are you facing one now or maybe you can see one on the horizon?

When you face these decisions, go straight to the Lord and ask for His help. He will know exactly what to do.

Complete these thoughts in your journal:

The most difficult decision I have ever faced is …

The toughest decision I am facing right now is …

Lord Jesus, please help me to know what I should do regarding …

When God shows up ...
love leads the lost
into the light.

MAKIN' SPACE FOR GRACE

S horty White, the head coach at Banks High, sits with Hank Erwin at a bar-b-que restaurant, devouring a plate of ribs. Coach Gerelds enters, shocked by the sight of these two men seated together, then even more surprised that Hank summoned him to meet them.

Shorty calls out, "Over here, Tandy." Gerelds sits down and reluctantly asks, "What's this about?" Shorty wipes sauce away from his mouth and answers, "We finally had our meeting—our tent revival thing. Jeff scheduled it at his church. Smart boy. Determined. I came again to stop it. Thought Jesus would make my boys weak. Well, wouldn't ya know I was the first one down the aisle? Cryin' like a child. My whole team followed me ... my whole team! Never seen anything like it. Don't know how it's even possible. How is that even possible? I'm here to tell you I'm a changed man and I wanna say 'I'm sorry.'"

The miracles just kept on coming. Hank's seeds of faith were now impacting Shorty and Banks' High. The revival was spreading. Change was coming.

Scripture speaks of forgiveness—and lack of it—often. When someone comes to Christ, getting relationships right, as much as is possible, is a by-product of redemption. Here are just a few samples of Jesus talking about forgiveness.

At that point Peter got up the nerve to ask, "Master, how many times do I forgive a brother or sister who hurts me? Seven?" Jesus replied, "Seven! Hardly. Try seventy times seven" (Matthew 18:21–22 MSG).

"And when you stand and pray, forgive anything you may have against anyone, so that your Father in heaven will forgive the wrongs you have done" (Mark 11:25 GNT).

So watch yourselves. "If your brother or sister sins against you, rebuke them; and if they repent, forgive them. Even if they sin against you seven times in a day and seven times come back to you saying 'I repent,' you must forgive them" (Luke 17:3–4 NIV).

Do you have a list of people who have hurt or wronged you (maybe not a literal list, but one you can call up in your mind, anytime you want)?

Are there people you stay angry with?

Is there someone you have a grudge against?

Is there anyone you are bitter toward?

Is there someone you actually hate?

Here are some easy identification triggers for answering these questions.

You can know you have a grudge when anytime you think of that person or someone mentions the person's name, you get angry—just like the day the offense occurred—or worse.

Bitterness has taken hold of you when you no longer have any interest or desire to reconcile with the person.

Hatred is in your heart when you no longer see any value in the person's life. This is exactly why hate is such a strong motive for murder.

Here are some practical steps for ridding yourself of unforgiveness, grudges, bitterness, and hatred.

1. Make a list by writing down the names of anyone in your life you feel has offended, wronged, or hurt you.

2. Pray for and about each person. Give the person and the situation to Jesus. Ask Him to take over and replace your anger with His love and forgiveness.

3. As the Lord leads and where it is possible, go to, call, or communicate with the people to ask for their forgiveness, and, where necessary, you forgive as well.

4. Once you work through your list, over the next few days, read it to check your thoughts and feelings. Do you sense you have experienced freedom when you read the names? There may be some situations where someone's actions have harmed you to the point that you may need professional counseling to find true healing. Get the help you need to get your heart right and pure.

5. Now that you have taken care of your list, keep it short! As soon as you feel anger toward someone, deal with the emotion and feeling right away. Go to God and work toward forgiveness, just as anytime you sin and confess; He forgives you.

Use today's journal entry to work through the above exercises.

ETERNAL EXCHANGE

Months later on Hank's suggestion, Coach Gerelds and Coach White decide to do summer football camp for the upcoming season a little differently than ever before. The two teams will come together to start their year. The busses pull into the university. Waiting there to meet them is Hank. The two teams pile out. Tony and Jeff Rutledge shake hands, as everyone looks to Hank.

The chaplain wastes no time jumping in. "Sometimes you have to be willing to be first. To do something no one has done before. To pave the way. That's what we're doing right here, right now." Tandy and Shorty are standing side by side, agreeing with the words.

As the teams begin to scrimmage, the two head coaches stand together in the crow's nest, positioned above their teams. Gerelds says to White, "I've always wanted two things professionally—to win a championship and coach a truly great player. You've done both. Which is better?" Shorty thoughtfully responds, "Rings collect dust." As he points out to the players on the field, he adds, "That right there. That lasts forever."

The two teams come together and circle up. Jeff and Tony lock arms, as both teams kneel to pray. This is a moment none of them will ever forget—especially the two coaches looking on, reflecting on all God has done in such a short time to change so many lives.

"Teacher, which is the most important commandment in the law of Moses?" Jesus replied, "'You must love the Lord your God with all your heart, all your soul, and all your mind.' This is the first and greatest commandment. A second is equally important: 'Love your neighbor as yourself'" (Matthew 22:36–39 NLT).

Have you ever thought about what we can take to heaven? Of course, we understand we can take nothing physical into a completely spiritual realm. But what of earth affects heaven?

Our impact for Christ on people—loving our neighbor through our love for Him—seems to be important to God here and in heaven. Simply put, our investment in people on earth affects heaven.

Please allow a little emotional and spiritual license here and imagine for a moment some potential encounters you might have in heaven with "your neighbors":

"Thanks for sharing and showing me Jesus for so many years."

"You told me about Christ but I just wasn't ready, and then years later, I heard the gospel again and remembered it matched with what you shared with me and I believed. Your words planted seeds for me down the road."

"I am here because you made sure I was fed every day far on the other side of the world, so I could stay alive and accept the Savior."

"Thanks for always being so kind and encouraging when you came through my line at the store. I knew you were different and it was a part of my journey that led me here."

"Thanks for all the many questions you answered about faith when I was struggling to believe."

If we really understood today that relationships with people—from family to the ten-second encounters in public, and each one in between—were all that truly mattered here for heaven, what difference would that make today in:

How much we ignore anyone?

How much we rush through conversations and transactions?

How much we focus on the little picture and miss the big one?

How many divine appointments we pass up, because we just aren't paying attention?

We live on a mission field everywhere we are, everywhere we go. God has placed us strategically where He wants us to share Him. And what can we take to heaven? The relationships we build today. The investments we make—in people's lives. To close with Shorty's words—"Rings (things) collect dust. That (relationships) lasts forever."

Take a few minutes to answer these questions in your journal:

- Where in your life might you be placing too much focus on a "ring"?

- Where in your life are you focused on relationships that will last forever?

- What is one step you can take to focus more on investments for heaven?

COURAGE VS. COWARDS

Tony is sitting at home in the family den, reading *Sports Illustrated*. There's a knock at the door. As he opens it up, there stands Coach Bear Bryant, holding a suitcase. Tony looks at it, then back at the coach. Bryant states, as only he could, "I'm not leavin' here until you decide to come to Alabama." He walks in past Tony, letting himself into the house with which he is now very familiar.

A bit later, they are all sitting at the dinner table. Momma Nathan sets a platter of food down in the middle of them all. Junior tells everyone to grab hands for the prayer. "Dear Lord, we thank You for this food and for Your provisions, for treatin' us with it, so that we might serve You."

After everyone says, "Amen," Coach Bryant decides to put in his own request. He respectfully states, "And may I add, 'God in heaven, help Tony see the light. Amen.'" Everyone laughs, but knows the coach is completely serious.

After the meal, Tony and Bear are sitting on the front porch. Bryant says, "Tony, the idea of molding men means a lot to me. I want you to know I'm here to help, no matter what choice you make and I'm thinkin' you can feel that." Tony stays silent.

Bear takes out a crumpled piece of paper and opens it. "Your momma showed me this. Said it was taped to a brick thrown into this house. Got somethin' to say to you, Son. You know the difference between you and those people?" Tony turns to hear the answer. Bear crumples the paper back up in his fist and states, "They're cowards. And you ain't."

Jesus had to deal with cowards on a regular basis in his life as well.

> Then the chief priests and the elders of the people assembled in the palace of the high priest, whose name was Caiaphas, and they schemed to arrest Jesus secretly and kill him. "But not during the festival," they said, "or there may be a riot among the people." … Then one of the Twelve— the one called Judas Iscariot—went to the chief priests and asked, "What are you willing to give me if I deliver him over to you?" So they counted out for him thirty pieces of silver. From then on Judas watched for an opportunity to hand him over (Matthew 26:3–5, 14–16 NIV).

When that brick came flying through Tony's window, it looked like the cowards were going to win. When Judas agreed to the chief priests' plot to hand over Jesus, it looked like the cowards were going to win. But God has a unique way of showing up just when things look their worst and begin to turn everything around. This was certainly the case at Woodlawn. To be a part of God's story requires a unique brand of courage.

The word "encouraging" means to give someone courage. Those who live courageously give courage to others. Here are ten differences between cowards and encouragers.

COWARDS	ENCOURAGERS
Curse others.	Bless others.
Burn bridges.	Build bridges.

COWARDS	ENCOURAGERS
Hit and run.	Run to help.
Live for self.	Live for others.
Operate out of fear.	Operate out of love.
Love tearing down.	Love building up.
Spout off.	Speak up.
Try to control.	Try to communicate.
Take what they want.	Give what you need.
Live in ignorance.	Live in integrity.

Based on this list of character qualities, do you need any adjustments to move toward being more of an encourager?

There is no doubt our current culture is growing more and more negative and hostile. Humans seem to find new ways every day to be nasty to each other. The Internet has bred a new brand of coward—anonymous, hiding behind a pseudonym.

As Christ followers, we must …

… maintain His character and not the culture's.

… be people known for giving courage to others.

… show cowards there is a better way to live.

Answer these questions in your journal:

- Which description on the "coward" side do you most struggle with?

- Which descriptions on the "encourager" side do you feel best describe you?

- What is one area you know you can improve in reflecting Christ through encouraging others?

When God shows up ...
the righteous rise up.

FRIDAY NIGHT LIGHTS

On this particular morning Tony doesn't run to his school, but goes to Legion field, the site designated for the play-off game. He's running the bleachers when he hears someone say, "Get those knees up." Tony stops to see Jeff Rutledge standing there.

"You spying out the battlefield like me? How many people, you think?" Jeff asks. Tony just shrugs. Jeff continues, "You see *Sports Illustrated*? "Nah, man," Tony answers. "The 'Faces in the Crowd' section. You're in there. Did Coach Bryant come see you yet?" "Yeah," Tony responds. "Did he give you the ring speech?" Tony just laughs and says, "Yes, he did." Jeff continues the questions, "You decided where you're going to college?" Tony answers, "Man, I don't even know."

Jeff offers confidently, "Go where you can make the most difference. That's what I'm gonna do. … Crazy all these people come to see us. What's so special about us?

Tony contemplates a moment, remembers what his dad told him and then answers, "Because we give them hope."

"Here's another way to put it: You're here to be light, bringing out the God-colors in the world. God is not a secret to be kept. We're going public with this, as public as a city on a hill. If I make you light-bearers, you don't think I'm going to hide you under a bucket, do you? I'm putting you on a light stand. Now that I've put you there on a hilltop, on a light stand—shine! Keep open house; be generous with your lives. By opening up to others, you'll prompt people to open up with God, this generous Father in heaven" (Matthew 5:14–16 MSG).

For Tony and Jeff, God was certainly "not a secret to be kept." Their lives and faith were on the line every day.

Notice Jesus did not say, "Find a city that is well-lit and move there," but rather "I've made you lights, so shine wherever you are." Jeff encouraged Tony to go where he could make the most difference. For Jeff, he wanted to go where his light would shine the brightest for Christ.

Think about the places and the people where you regularly spend time. How would you rate those places on their level of "darkness?" When you are in each of those settings, how bright do you shine for Christ and how are you bringing hope to others?

Consider these points of encouragement for your own life.

1. God has placed you right where you are to bring His light into darkness and His hope to the hopeless. It is often tempting for Christians to move away from all points of darkness to just be with other lights. Of course, if there is a consistent place of darkness that is hurting you or creating a place of sin, you must leave, but this truth is an inspiration for you to shine your light into any dark place where God has placed you.

2. Light is the only force that can dispel darkness. Light always overcomes darkness. No one has ever said, "Hey, would you turn on the darkness?" That is not even possible and also ridiculous to ask. No, if in a dark room with someone, we ask, "Would you please turn on the light?"

3. Even a tiny candle flame becomes the focus in a vast room full of darkness. Right at dawn, when the sun peeks over the horizon, what do we focus on—the darkness still lingering or the sunrise? Always the light. We often feel we are not making a difference in the world, but even a small light can be seen, appreciated, and used for long distances.

One of the best ways to bring more light into our own lives is to constantly be light to others. One of the best ways to keep hope alive in our own hearts is to consistently bring hope to others. The ability to shine for Christ is what makes you special too, just like Tony was talking about.

In your journal, write down:

- a dark place where you know you have been placed.

- a place you frequently find yourself where there may already be too many lights.

- a place you sense God calling you to bring His hope.

WHEN GOD
SHOWS UP

One evening in Legion Stadium, Hank Erwin walks to the microphone in front of the three thousand students gathered. He begins, "I want to thank Coach Gerelds and his team for putting this together. Look around you. Look at this! Can you believe it?! This is what happens when God shows up!" The students cheer.

"A couple of years back, I went to something called *Explo '72* in Dallas where I joined a hundred thousand people just like us. Up until that time in my life I had felt so insignificant. I felt like I didn't matter. Then on the last night, they shut the lights off in the Cotton Bowl—just like this."

At that moment, the massive floodlights in the stadium all shut off. Only a single, small light remains on Hank. He continues, "And in the darkness, Reverend Billy Graham lit one single candle. I was standing in the very back of the Cotton Bowl, but I could see that light … that one single light … and I realized." As Hank pauses, tears well up in his eyes, then he shares, "I realized in that moment, I was not insignificant."

Mike Allyson lights a single candle in the middle of the crowd. He then lights the candle of the person next to him. That person then lights another's candle. And so on it goes. The light begins to spread and faces begin to shine.

Hank continues, "One candle became two, which became

ten, which became a hundred thousand, all burning as one. People in Dallas started calling the police saying that the Cotton Bowl was on fire because of the fiery glow." He pauses. "And you know what ... they were right!"

As the light from hundreds of candles begins to fill the scene with an amber glow, Hank says, "*Time* magazine wrote about us a couple years back. They said the 'Jesus Revolution,' as they called it, had a symbol." Hank raises his fist in the air with his index finger upward. The crowd begins to shout. As Tony and Johnnie are sitting together, she puts her hand in the air, matching his gesture.

Hank boldly states, "This is our symbol, because there is one way. One way! You're here united, not by the name of your teams or schools but by the Name that is above all names—Jesus!"

The students' cheers grow louder, as Hank concludes, "One person—alone in the dark—willing to speak the truth when it's not popular. One person—willing to speak the truth when it's not safe—when there is much at stake. Look around you. We are not alone. This is what happens when God shows up!"

The Message is as true among you today as when you first heard it. It doesn't diminish or weaken over time. It's the same all over the world. The Message bears fruit and gets larger and stronger, just as it has in you (Colossians 1:5–6 MSG).

God is always at work, constantly moving behind the scenes and accomplishing His purposes. His kingdom advances, reaching around the world, growing "larger and stronger."

When you continue to pray, but see nothing, keep seeking Him. He is at work.

When you are being obedient, but see no blessing yet, keep

being faithful to Him. He will make every moment worth the wait.

When you read your Bible and it begins to feel stale, keep reading, because He is storing His Word in your heart for a greater purpose to come.

When you are sharing your faith with a friend or family member, but he/she is not responding, keep sharing. God is moving in his/her heart.

When life is getting tough and everyone seems to be against you, keep walking in the light of Christ. He will see you through and bring you out the other side, better and stronger.

When you feel completely alone, stay close to Jesus and keep following. Pass the test. In His time, He will bring you far more than you could ever ask or imagine.

In your journal, write down:

- a prayer you have given up on that you need to pray once again.

- an area of obedience you need to get serious about once again.

- the name of a person you most want to see come to know Christ.

Take a few moments to pray about each of the answers you've written down.

When God shows up ...
love lightens the load.

FATHER FAVOR

Woodlawn versus Banks—November 8, 1974—winner take all. The stadium is packed, turning people away. The highest attended high school football game in Alabama history.

"Coach, could I have a minute with my son?" Junior asks Coach Gerelds in the locker room. He nods approval.

"Lotta people out there, Dad," Tony says, as Junior turns to sit down in front of his son. Knowing the weight of this moment, the father responds, "I know. But they're not here to see Woodlawn versus Banks. They're here to see you. Tony, you've given a lot of people hope and I'm proud of you. But I don't really care what happens out there. Win or lose ..." Junior leans forward and looks deep into Tony's eyes. "You're my son." Junior takes his hand and allows the blessing to sink in.

Many sons and daughters have never heard, and never will hear, a blessing like the one Junior gave to Tony. A moment alone with a dad, simply to look deep into the eyes and communicate, "I'm proud of you and I love you no matter what you do, just because you are my child." These are words everyone longs to hear, but too few ever do.

Here's a basic biology fact—every human who has ever been on this planet began life with a father and a mother. While many children know their parents, some never do. Circumstances cause some children to never know one or both of their parents. But God uses a man and a woman to create children, so we all start our lives with parents, no matter how long they may stay in our lives. Regardless of your own relationship with your family, a relationship with your heavenly Father is available to you with no limit to His love, approval, and acceptance.

> Think how much the Father loves us. He loves us so much that he lets us be called his children, as we truly are. But since the people of this world did not know who Christ is, they don't know who we are. My dear friends, we are already God's children, though what we will be hasn't yet been seen. But we do know that when Christ returns, we will be like him, because we will see him as he truly is. This hope makes us keep ourselves holy, just as Christ is holy (1 John 3:1–3 CEV).

After you accept Christ, two processes occur between God, the Father, and you as His child.

First, you are adopted—officially and forever. You take Jesus' name as your own and His blood begins to course through your veins. Just as when parents adopt a child through the court system take on all responsibility for the child, God takes on full responsibility of you.

Second, after you are adopted by God, you begin the lifelong process of taking on Christ's character. Like a child begins to mimic the qualities of his/her parents, you begin to think like and act like Jesus. The only thing you can control is the speed at which you change, because obedience to conform to Christ is in your court. But His character and fruit are made available to you the moment He takes over.

Because of this adoption and this growth plan, when Jesus

returns there will be an immediate and unmistakable unity between the Father and His children.

I don't know how you imagine the second coming of Christ, but think about this scene for a moment. All the kids in a home are sitting at the window, waiting on dad to get there. He pulls in the driveway and every one of them jumps up, runs out the door to hug him, and welcome him back. Now that is a great picture of the second coming, as God's children await His return.

Today, regardless of the relationship you had, have, or didn't with your earthly father, know that your heavenly Father looks at you and says, "I'm proud of you and I love you no matter what you do, just because you are My child."

In your journal, prayerfully answer these questions:

- What are a few descriptive words of how you view God as your Father?

- What steps can you take to receive and accept God's approval of you? How can you let His love sink deeper into your soul?

- Is there someone in your own life who needs to hear these same words of acceptance and blessing? If so, why wait? Plan to share with him/her this week.

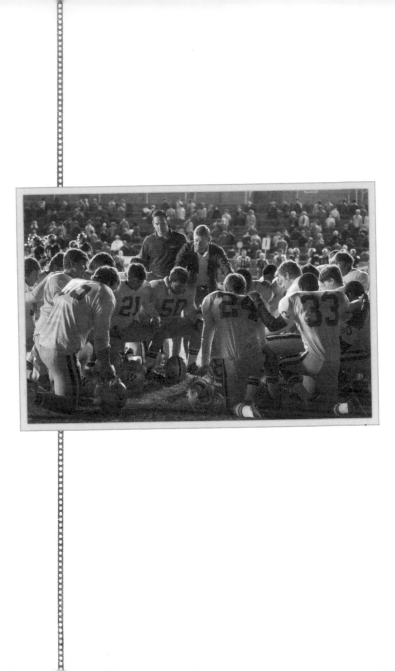

SPEAKING
YOUR HEART

Legion Field is full to capacity. Coach Bear Bryant and six other SEC coaches line the press box. The teams take the field and "The Star Bangled Banner" is sung. Coach Gerelds looks at Hank and says, "Let's go, Hank." Hank looks puzzled and asks, "Where we going?" "To do something wild and rebellious," Gerelds answers, smiling.

Coach Gerelds walks with Hank onto the middle of the field. He calls for Shorty White, Banks' head coach and new brother in Christ, to join them. Gerelds says to Erwin, "Pray for us, Hank." Hank, unsure, asks, "Really?" The coach nods confidently and says, "Pray for us."

Shorty jogs to midfield and asks, "What are we doing?" Hank replies, "Giving credit where credit's due." Coach White removes his cap and says, "Then let's pray."

Hank walks to the microphone and asks the capacity crowd, "Will you pray with me?" The school superintendant is enraged. He begins to run up the bleachers to the press box, as the crowd stands to its feet.

Erwin begins, "Our Father, who art in heaven, hallowed be Thy name. Thy kingdom come, Thy will …" At that moment, the superintendant gets to the sound system and yanks the cord for the microphone out of the sound board.

Hank abruptly stops, uncertain of what has happened. The coaches look around. Just then the three realize the crowd is continuing the prayer. Coaches, players, referees, and the entire crowd have joined in.

"Forgive us of our trespasses as we forgive those who trespass against us. And lead us not into temptation but deliver us from evil. For Thine is the kingdom and the power and the glory forever. Amen." At the close, the crowd cheers.

As the two coaches smile and run to their sidelines, Hank, still in awe, shakes his head and says, "Amen."

The truth is, in a crowd of thousands reciting the Lord's Prayer, there would be some who would be praying fervently, while others are just recalling a childhood memory from church. Some would be radically praying, others religiously rambling, and still others respectfully reciting.

If you ask the average busy Christian today, "Do you believe in the power of prayer?" the answer would likely be, "Yes. Absolutely!" Then ask, "Do you believe laying your cares and burdens before the Lord, plus interceding for those around you, is an important priority?" Again, the answer would be "Certainly."

Then the next question, "Does the time you spend daily, weekly, in prayer reflect your belief in this spiritual discipline you feel so strongly about?" This is the point where so many of us start to be convicted.

Maybe when you began this devotional book, it had been a while since you've prayed or you know you've just not been engaged the way you want to be. Maybe you are a devout prayer warrior. Regardless of where you are in your commitment to spend time in prayer, here are a few thoughts to remind us of the basic discipline of prayer.

1. **Prayer is a conversation between you and your heavenly Father.**

2. **Your Father wants to hear your heart.**

3. **Your Father wants you to be specific about what you need.**

Basic and simple, right? If you've made your prayer time into anything else, maybe this would be a good time to get back to the simplicity of the conversation. For a reason higher than we can understand, Scripture is quite clear on God asking for us to tell Him what, in His sovereignty, He already knows about us. And that can only be for one reason—He desires a relationship with us as His children—a talk-and-listen, give-and-take friendship.

Today could be a great moment for many of us to humbly hit our knees and reacquaint ourselves with, not only a simple, heart-felt prayer, but also a renewal of a heart-connected relationship with our heavenly Father.

> "God will always give what is right to his people who cry to him night and day, and he will not be slow to answer them. I tell you, God will help his people quickly. But when the Son of Man comes again, will he find those on earth who believe in him?" (Luke 18:7–8 NCV).

In your journal, take a few moments and write out a prayer like a short letter to your Father Who deeply loves you.

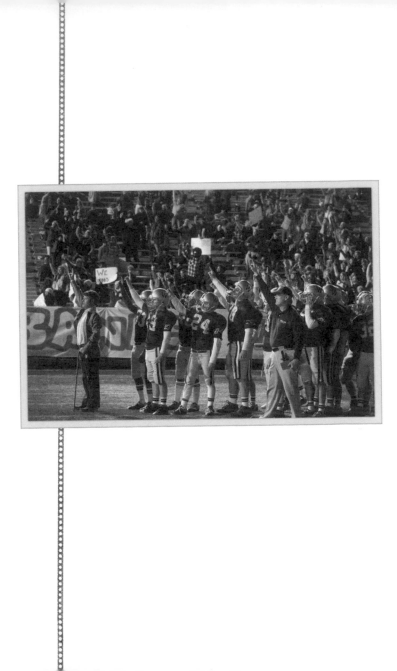

GOAL-LINE GLORY

The gridiron showdown between Woodlawn and Banks High has roared to life. On every play, every player is giving their all. While showing no mercy between the whistles, the spirit of Christ is clearly visible in the coaches and players' attitudes and actions.

Banks' quarterback Jeff Rutledge is finally able to get a drive going and they score. Woodlawn then gets the ball back, but is clearly struggling. Coach Gerelds calls time out and motions for the offense, pulling them to the sideline. "Boys, take a breath. Just breathe. Look around you. Savor this moment. Okay, I-right twenty five blast. Let's go do it."

As the players run back onto the field, Gerelds calls out. "Nathan!" Tony stops and turns back. "What do you feel but can't say? What do you want to tell these people? You say it when you run, Tony. You say it when … you … run!" as he points to the field. "Now, this is your moment. Your time. Go take it! You go and take it!"

Tony charges out, now calm with a sudden sense of peace overcoming him. He looks around toward all the people he loves. His parents. Cedric. Johnnie. His fellow teammates, his new brothers in Christ, even Coach Bryant in the press box.

Tony takes the hand-off, spinning and leaping over defenders, sprinting for the sideline. He turns on the speed. There is no catching him. But, in this moment, it's not about his ability or skill. That isn't what he wants everyone to know. As he runs down the sideline, he puts his fist into the air and points toward heaven. He may be running for a touchdown, but God will get the glory tonight. This is far bigger than football.

Cedric jumps to his feet and puts his hand into the air too, pointing to heaven. Others stand and begin to join in. As Tony crosses the goal line, he turns around toward the crowd. With the football in one hand, he keeps his other in the air, pointing upward. The other players and hundreds of fans join him in the gesture of worship. Even Banks' players and Coach White take part in the praise. Like a tidal wave washing over the crowd, all over the stadium, more and more stand and join in with hands in the air. You can feel the awe and reverence from all that God had done in their midst and how far He had brought so many out of hatred and anger to love and unity. The unlikely place of a football field under the Friday night lights had become a sanctuary filled with the glory of God.

The year King Uzziah died I saw the Lord! He was sitting on a lofty throne, and the Temple was filled with his glory. ... In a great antiphonal chorus they sang, "Holy, holy, holy is the Lord Almighty; the whole earth is filled with his glory." Such singing it was! It shook the Temple to its foundations, and suddenly the entire sanctuary was filled with smoke. Then I said, "My doom is sealed, for I am a foul-mouthed sinner, a member of a sinful, foul-mouthed race; and I have looked upon the King, the Lord of heaven's armies." Then one of the mighty angels flew over to the altar and with a pair of tongs picked out a burning coal. He touched my lips with it and said,

"Now you are pronounced 'not guilty' because this coal has touched your lips. Your sins are all forgiven." Then I heard the Lord asking, "Whom shall I send as a messenger to my people? Who will go?" And I said, "Lord, I'll go! Send me" (Isaiah 6:1, 3–8 TLB).

The coaches, players, and all those impacted by the movement of God at Woodlawn and Banks had clearly seen what their sin was capable of. Everyone was sick of the hurt, pain, and divisiveness. The depth of their pain helped them see the power of Christ.

The only possible and proper response to a holy God Who has freed, redeemed, and forgiven us is to answer His call with "Lord, I will go! Send me."

In your journal today, write down:

- any barrier keeping you from obeying God to go where He wants you to go.

- where you believe God wants to send you.

- to whom you believe God wants to send you.

When God shows up ...
        lives are liberated.

MIRACLE MOMENTS

"It was amazing. You could feel it in the stadium all over. 42,000 fans at a high school football game. Not even the play-offs. None of the tickets were prepurchased. They had to send home 20,000 people. A *National Geographic* reporter was traveling through and even wrote about us. Called it undeniably spiritual. Supernatural even. It was life changing for me."

A customer is hanging on every word from Tandy, as he has been answering the client's questions about the glory days of Woodlawn. Gerelds sits across from him in a button-up, short-sleeve shirt and tie. A nametag is pinned on his shirt pocket, looking like an insurance salesman should. Since he's no longer a coach.

The man leans in closer and asks, "So?" … "So what?" Tandy asks back. "Did you win?" the man inquires. Gerelds laughs and answers, "No. No, we didn't. … Look, I'll have this policy ready for you first thing in the morning. No problem." As Tandy pushes back the desk chair and stands, the customer is still not focused on his insurance, but Tandy's story. "So what's your answer? … Do you believe in miracles?" Without pause, Gerelds responds, "Yes I do. I am one."

As Tandy walks out of the office, he looks across the street to Woodlawn High School. A group of kids are playing touch football on the front lawn. Blacks and whites … together.

Having a blast. The way kids should; the way they were meant to be.

For those who choose God, we are all one family with one Father. Much like those kids playing in the front of Woodlawn. And the team Tandy had coached in that incredible season.

> So from now on, we do not think about what people are like by looking at them. We even thought about Christ that way one time. But we do not think of Him that way anymore. For if a man belongs to Christ, he is a new person. The old life is gone. New life has begun. All this comes from God. He is the One Who brought us to Himself when we hated Him. He did this through Christ. Then He gave us the work of bringing others to Him (2 Corinthians 5:16–18 NLV).

These verses well describe the transformation the Woodlawn football team had gone through. The gospel literally changed everything and defeated every foe they faced. And now, Tandy Gerelds' life was completely transformed. He could see the change he and his team had brought to the community right there on the front lawn of the school.

When Jesus comes into our lives, He gives us …

1. A different place to look. The love and mercy of Christ gives us a higher standard to which we may look—not to culture, the government, or any particular group of people, agenda, or tangent. We keep our eyes on God and His ways. We look to Him and He helps us see ourselves, others, situations, and the world through the proper lens.

Our eyes look to God, not at the circumstances. We look

up to Him, not down on people. His Spirit allows us to see life through His eyes.

2. A different way to think. For Woodlawn High, the mindset was focused on two things—color and control. The FBI was even brought in to keep things in check. Minds had to be changed. Hearts had to be made right. The negatives had to be turned to positives. Ignorance had to be replaced with knowledge. Cynicism had to be replaced with hope. The eternal had to overpower the temporary. Love had to reign over hatred.

When Christ enters our hearts, His love begins to infiltrate our minds and thoughts. This teaches us a new and different way to think.

3. A different life to live. At Woodlawn, unity overcame chaos. Life ruled over death. Winning overcame losing. The old lives the players and coaches had lived were forever gone; the new had indeed come! Life was no longer about every man for himself, but focused on loving neighbors—all of them.

As a Christian, you are in a new place, living a new way, and having a new life. Where and what we look to. How we think. And how we live. Christ changes everything.

In your journal, write out how Christ has given you:

- a new place to look.
- a new way to think.
- a new life to live.

LEAVING
A LASTING LEGACY

Tandy Gerelds has just finished watching the Sugar Bowl—
January 1979. The University of Alabama with Jeff Rutledge
at quarterback and Tony Nathan at tailback has just defeated
Penn State 14–7. He walks into his study, looking over a wall
full of his old football pictures. The phone on his desk begins to
ring, startling him out of his reminiscing. He answers, "Hello."
Tony is on the other end. "Hey, Coach. Told you I'd win you a
championship." The words are a complete surprise. "Tony?"

Tony is standing in the tunnel at the Sugar Bowl on a pay phone.
He couldn't wait to call the man who started it all, took the risk,
and believed in him. He asks Gerelds, "Did you see it?" Gerelds
answers, "Wouldn't have missed it for the world. So proud of you."

Tony continues, "Don't have much time but I wanted to tell
you somethin'. I'm askin' Johnnie to marry me after graduation."
"Tony, that's just great. Congratulations." "How's the team this
year?" Tony asks. Gerelds says, "Oh. I'm not coaching anymore.
Needed some time away. Selling insurance now. Right across
the street from Woodlawn. It … ah … gives me a lot more time
with my family." Tony, a little disappointed, but understanding, says, "All right. I respect that. They callin' for me. I gotta
go." After a moment of silence, Tony says, "I love you, Coach."
Gerelds tears up, pauses then responds, "I love you too, Son."

Not missing a beat, Tony says, "I don't know what kinda

insurance salesman you are, but you were born to be a coach. One of the the best I've ever played for. Someone once told me we all have a purpose. Maybe it's time to start living yours again."

As the two say good-bye and Gerelds hangs up the phone, he looks again at the many pictures on his wall. He removes his sales nametag and reaches for something he hasn't had on in quite a while. Looking at the picture of the 1973 Woodlawn team, he smiles, and puts on his coaching cap.

Tandy Gerelds returned to coaching at Deschler High School. He won 110 games in ten seasons and won a state championship in 1990.

Tony played for the Miami Dolphins for ten years and became an NFL running back coach. He and Johnnie have been married for over thirty-five years.

As iron sharpens iron, so a friend sharpens a friend (Proverbs 27:17 NLT).

This popular verse is often quoted and used in many settings, but there is a deeper meaning to be found here.

The usual coach and player relationship is the coach pouring in knowledge, hoping to see the player excel at his position. The player receives and then sets out to apply it to experience glory on the field. For thousands upon thousands of coaches and players, the only end goal is winning.

But with a small number, as was true with Coach Gerelds and Tony Nathan, it goes past the role and the uniform to the heart and soul. Love, respect, and genuine care became the overriding force over winning and losing. This is the heart of Proverbs 27:17. When two pieces of iron or blades scrape and collide together, both will be sharpened. The process impacts each, not just the one needing the most honing.

Now that you have successfully navigated these forty days of devotionals, where do you want to go? How do you want to see your life change? If you've seen the need for a course correction in your faith, how can you insure you'll take the right road and truly go to a new place?

1. Keep God first. Seek Him first in all things. Keep a constant conversation going with Him. Listen to His voice. Rest in His presence.

2. Find your iron. We must find those people who will sharpen us in our faith; inspire and encourage spiritual growth; challenge us to reach for our dreams and not settle.

3. Be iron. God didn't create you for status quo, but to be all He gifted you to become. He has a calling, a mission, and a purpose that only you can fulfill. You are the only you He made and there is a reason for that so you can reach your world.

After his final season of coaching, Coach Tandy Gerelds died of cancer in 2003. Over a thousand people attended his funeral. While death is a subject we often avoid, it can be a positive motivation to think about our legacy.

What would we like for people to remember us for? To get to the place we hope for in how we are remembered, we must begin here in this life.

Right here, right now, change begins with you!

SHOW THE WORLD WHAT CAN HAPPEN … WHEN GOD SHOWS UP!

In your final journal entry, take a few minutes and write out some simple goals for how you can become "iron" and leave a lasting legacy for Christ.

WHEN GOD SHOWS UP— IN YOUR LIFE!

Congratulations on completing the forty days of devotions in this book! All of us involved with this project pray you now know what life can be like when God shows up every day because you are inviting Him to work in and through your life.

We want to encourage you to continue your new habit of spending time with God daily—reading his Word, praying, listening, applying, and growing in your faith. Then taking all He gives you and reaching your world for Christ—just as Hank Erwin did in starting a revival that spread over two high school campuses and beyond in Birmingham.

God can and wants to bring a new revolution of redemption to the land and He wants you to join Him in His work. So stand strong and show the world what can happen—when God shows up!

I pray that from his glorious, unlimited resources he will empower you with inner strength through his Spirit. Then Christ will make his home in your hearts as you trust in him. Your roots will grow down into God's love and keep you strong. And may you have the power to understand, as all God's people should, how wide, how long, how high, and how deep his love is. May you experience the love of Christ, though it is too great to understand fully. Then you will be made complete with all the fullness of life and power that comes from God. Now all glory to God, who is able, through his mighty power at work within us, to accomplish infinitely more than we might ask or think. Glory to him in the church and in Christ Jesus through all generations forever and ever! Amen (Ephesians 3:16–21 NLT).

ABOUT THE AUTHOR

Robert Noland began his writing career as a songwriter in 1983, penning lyrics for artists such as Glen Campbell, Babbie Mason, Paul Smith, and Gabriel. He then spent the next 10 years as a touring musician and producer. He wrote his first series of Bible studies in 1988 and in 1991 wrote his first Christian devotional book for a para-church ministry.

Noland has since authored over 60 titles spanning across children, youth, and adult audiences. In 1996, he wrote a Christian follow-up booklet entitled *LifeChange*, published by *Student Discipleship Ministries*, which to date has sold over one million copies.

In 2010, he released his first book, *The Knight's Code*, along with *3SG, Men's Small Group Manual* through his own ministry *517 Resources, Inc.* Robert regularly blogs at *theknightscode.com* and speaks at Christian men's events.

Since 2011, he has been a free-lance writer and editor for Christian publishers, ministries, and faith-based organizations. Recent projects where Robert has contributed his writing and editing include.

—*Facts & Trends* magazine (LifeWay 2014-2015)

—*Think, Act, Believe Like Jesus*, Randy Frazee, Zondervan 2014

—*Do You Believe? 40 Day Devotional, (*From the *Pure Flix* film, *Do You Believe?),* Broadstreet 2015

—*When God Shows Up: 40 Day Devotional* (From the Jon and Andy Erwin film *Woodlawn)*, Broadstreet 2015

—*Living Among Lions,* David & Jason Benham, *W Publishing* 2016

—*How to Live in Fear,* Lance Hahn, *W Publishing* 2016

Regardless of the target audience or mode of delivery via paper or digital, Robert writes what he calls, "practical application of Biblical truth." He lives in Franklin, Tennessee with his wife of 30+ years and has two adult sons.

Visit his web site at robertnoland.com.

ONE HOPE.
ONE DREAM.
ONE WAY.
PUREFLIX PRESENTS
AN ERWIN BROTHERS FILM
WOODLAWN
THE TRUE STORY
IN THEATERS
OCTOBER 16